P9-CRZ-331

Praise for VEGAN with a VENGEANCE

"It's hip. It's punk. It's high energy. And it's darn fun to read! Cohost of a community-access vegan cooking show called *The Post Punk Kitchen*, Moskowitz here espouses a philosophy of being kind to both animals and one's budget and of adopting a do-it-yourself attitude for a fun time in the kitchen. *Vegan* has a solid repertoire of recipes that will carry readers through the day, the seasons, and the holidays. Even though everything is made from scratch, most of the recipes are neither complicated nor time-consuming. The ingredients are common enough to be found in most large grocery stores or health food stores, and Moskowitz encourages substitution and experimentation. She provides good, basic information about handling tofu and making seitan and includes sidebars, a.k.a. 'Punk Points,' with tips ranging from how to purée soup in a blender to how to cook with lemongrass. And who can resist a vegan cookbook with recipes for Hazelnut Scones or Brooklyn Pad Thai that yield excellent results? This book will be a hit with teens and young adults as well as with adults wanting to add more spice to their own kitchen experiments. Highly recommended for all public libraries."

—*LIBRARY JOURNAL*, starred review

"This is not your mother's cookbook. *Vegan with a Vengeance* has got plenty of attitude, and killer recipes to back it up. Watch out, Betty Crocker. Isa's coming to kick your ass."

—ERIK MARCUS, author of *Meat Market—Animals, Ethics, and Money*, publisher of Vegan.com

"Good, honest vegan recipes with broad appeal."

—*ASSOCIATED PRESS*

"Rise up domesticated thirty-something punk rockers! We may not be dyeing our hair purple or accessorizing with safety pins and duct tape anymore, but we're still creating culture with the same feisty D.I.Y. ethic as when we booked our first basement show (sorry Mom!) or photocopied our first zine. *Vegan with a Vengeance* artfully integrates Isa's New York and punk roots with a sophisticated culinary palate and political nuance that only comes with experience—all served up with humor and attitude."

—Josh Hooten, *Herbivore* magazine

"If you're sick of feeding corporate giants while you feed yourself, Isa's book is the best place to start. Food doesn't have to be filled with preservatives, injected with hormones, painted artificial colors, and wrapped in plastic to taste good. *Vegan with a Vengeance* shows you can make great, healthy food and still live with yourself in the morning."

—Jim Lindberg, Pennywise

"A vegetarian since her teens, Moskowitz's philosophy about food can be summed up by the words 'cooking is fun.' If your only frame of reference for vegans is the type of activist who's decked out in an Anna Wintour mask outside the Condé Nast building or protesting against Perdue, think again. Moskowitz is likely to get chefs and non-chefs, vegans and meat-eaters alike salivating over scrumptious-sounding recipes. . . . Prepare to have your appetite whetted."

—Gothamist.com

"This is, hands down, the most kick-ass vegan cookbook ever. We're going to buy copies for everyone we know so there's never any doubt as to how well vegans eat."

—Bob and Jenna Torres, authors of
Vegan Freak: Being Vegan in a Non-Vegan World

"A chatty Brooklynite who hosts her own public access cooking show, [Moskowitz] scatters stories about her mother, her friends, and her politics among recipes for goodies like Fresh Corn Fritters and Curried Split Pea Soup. . . . BBQ Pomegranate Tofu is actually baked, not barbecued, but still the tofu is rich and smoky, terrific over rice or packed into heroes. Even better, the vegan iterations of Spanakopita and Seitan-Portobello Stroganoff so closely approximate the traditional versions that even the pickiest eaters would happily trade one for the other. And although there's no chicken broth in Matzoh Ball Soup, the vegetable stock is hearty enough to cure the fiercest cold. Best of all, and rare in a vegan cookbook, the author provides several appealing dairy-free desserts that are tasty enough to fool most omnivores, yet unique enough to thrill any vegan who just can't face another tofu ice cream bar."

—*Publishers Weekly*

DISCARDED

DALY CITY PUBLIC LIBRARY
DALY CITY, CALIFORNIA

VEGAN

WITH A VENGEANCE

Over 150 Delicious, Cheap, Animal-Free Recipes That Rock

Isa Chandra Moskowitz

Photographs by Geoffrey Tischman

Food styling by Neje Bailey, isa Chandra Moskowitz, and Terry Romero

B

641.5636
mos

Many of the designations used by manufacturers and sellers to distinguish their products are claimed as trademarks. Where those designations appear in this book and Da Capo Press was aware of a trademark claim, the designations have been printed in initial capital letters.

Copyright © 2005 by Isa Chandra Moskowitz
Foreword copyright © 2005 by Ryan MacMichael
Photographs copyright © 2005 by Geoffrey Tischman

All rights reserved. No part of this publication may be reproduced, stored in a retrieval system, or transmitted, in any form or by any means, electronic, mechanical, photocopying, recording, or otherwise, without the prior written permission of the publisher. Printed in the United States of America. For information, address Da Capo Press, 11 Cambridge Center, Cambridge, MA 02142.

Designed by Pauline Neuwirth, Neuwirth & Associates, Inc.
Set in 11.5 point Whitman LF by the Perseus Books Group

Cataloging-in-Publication data for this book is available from the Library of Congress.

ISBN: 978-1-56924-358-9

Published by Da Capo Press
A Member of the Perseus Books Group
www.dacapopress.com

Note: The information in this book is true and complete to the best of our knowledge. This book is intended only as an informative guide for those wishing to know more about health issues. In no way is this book intended to replace, countermand, or conflict with the advice given to you by your own physician. The ultimate decision concerning care should be made between you and your doctor. We strongly recommend you follow his or her advice. Information in this book is general and is offered with no guarantees on the part of the authors or Da Capo Press. The authors and publisher disclaim all liability in connection with the use of this book. The names and identifying details of people associated with events described in this book have been changed. Any similarity to actual persons is coincidental.

Da Capo Press books are available at special discounts for bulk purchases in the U.S. by corporations, institutions, and other organizations. For more information, please contact the Special Markets Department at the Perseus Books Group, 2300 Chestnut Street, Suite 200, Philadelphia, PA, 19103, or call (800) 810-4145, extension 5000, or e-mail special.markets@perseusbooks.com.

20 19 18 17 16 15 14 13

Dedicated to my mom, Marlene Stewart, RN:
The most kick-ass nurse and mother NYC has ever known.

My first thank-you is for Justin; for typing, prepping, listening, going to the store, cleaning up after me, and ghostwriting the entire book for me while I lay in my hammock and fanned myself. Well, not quite, but still.

My testers—Jennifer Philburn, Adam Nelson, Jo Scovell, Drew Blood, Chris Poupart, Carrie Lynn Reilly, Paula Gross, Justin Walsh, Dominique Ryder, Kittee Berns, and Lynda Bartram. Not a day went by when I didn't check our testing site and think that you guys were awesome.

Terry Hope Romero, my partner in crime.

Denise Gaberman, Niharika Desai, and Lou Thomas for being part of *Post Punk Kitchen* and helping to make the most awesomest vegan cooking show in the world—without which there would be no cookbook.

Michelle Moskowitz Brown, for inspiring me and giving me honest feedback. Thanks to her hubby, Aaron, just because, and of course my nephew Maxwell Aaron Brown for being a beautiful baby. See Max? Tanta Isa put you in a book!

Erica Rose Levine, even though she didn't do anything she is my best friend and would kill me if I didn't thank her. Oh, she let me stay at her house and write so scratch that. And Amy Sims for proofreading things via Instant Messenger during the wee hours of the morning.

Michael Robert Cooper aka Mumbles for workshopping with me and being the wind beneath my wings (literally).

Geoffery Tischman for working with my crazy schedule and taking such beautiful photographs.

Marlowe & Company: Kylie Foxx for bearing with me through a computer meltdown and nervous breakdown, and Matthew Lore for accepting my proposal.

My literary agent—Marc Gerald at the Agency Group. Thanks for believing in me and realizing the potential my little idea had.

And lastly thanks to all the zines and Web sites that supported me and got the word out about *The Post Punk Kitchen*: *Punk Planet*, *Herbivore* magazine, *Satya* magazine, *Bust* magazine, *Venus* magazine, Nerdnyc.com, Vegblog.org, and Veganfreaks.org especially.

contents

VEGAN WITH A VENGEANCE

Cookies and Bars [191]

Desserts [213]

index [247]

VEGAN WITH A VENGEANCE

foreword

by Ryan MacMichael, vegblog.org

I'M ABOUT AS far removed from being "punk" as one can be. Or at least, I look that way. I'm more of a . . . how do you say? . . . a nerd. But one part of the punk aesthetic I've always connected with is the idea of "Do It Yourself." Whether it's in relation to music, publishing, or cooking, the unpolished, improvised nature of DIY projects results in something much more interesting than most overtly commercial efforts.

Vegetarians and vegans have long adopted the DIY philosophy because, let's face it, we don't live in a very vegan world. We have to be constantly creative, finding ways to adapt to situations that clearly don't have animals (or animal-friendly humans) in mind. And, really, the only thing more creative than trying to form a vegan meal out of side dishes at a diner in rural Kentucky is creating a new recipe from fresh, locally grown ingredients or adapting a childhood favorite like Lard-Covered Lardballs Simmered in Lard-Enhanced Lard. Actually, that last thing probably wouldn't be possible. Well, if you substituted Crisco for the lard and homemade seitan for the lard, then *maybe* . . .

Never mind.

Vegan with a Vengeance has succeeded in not only bringing vegan cooking home, but bringing home cooking to vegans. Isa Chandra Moskowitz's recipes are both exotically creative and comfortingly accessible. Her avoidance of prepared convenience foods will help wean you from the corporate teat while at the same time saving you money and encouraging you to support local growers.

As you flip through the book you'll find that you come across recipes you've never seen before (BBQ Pomegranate Tofu) as well as fresh takes on old favorites (Scrambled Tofu). And this may be the first vegetarian cookbook ever that doesn't have a single salad recipe.

Isa has kindly laid out what you need in your kitchen to be a successful at-home vegan chef, both the equipment in your cupboards/on your walls and the food in your pantry. If she can film a cooking show in her tiny Brooklyn kitchen, you'll be able to stock up on the bare essentials with no problems.

But the creativity doesn't end with the recipes. You'll get ideas about starting a brunch café (hint: Isa never once mentions anything about registering as an LLC or the intricacies of business finance), buying kitchen equipment without electrocuting yourself, and reading up on veganism on "teh Intarweb." Thanks to Isa's cat, Fizzle, I'm now well versed in food history. And I've accumulated enough "punk point" cooking tips that I'm hoping to cash them in for something more punk than my current buttondown work shirt.

Eating is a moral act or a political statement, depending on whom you ask. When you choose to stop eating animal products and supporting big business, you prove both statements to be correct. *Vegan with a Vengeance* will make that a lot easier. And it also helps me feel a little more punk.

What It's All About

WELCOME TO *Vegan with a Vengeance*! Here you'll find a collection of vegan recipes that I've created over the past sixteen years. Some recipes I dreamed up, some are classic favorites that I veganized, and some are dishes inspired by food that I've eaten at restaurants and just had to make for myself. Since the book says VEGAN in really big letters on the front cover and you probably wouldn't have picked it up if you weren't interested in vegan cooking, I am going to guess that you know all about veganism and think it's just great. So I am going to skip the song and dance about how healthy, ethical, and fun veganism can be.

I cook because I love to eat, it's as simple as that. But why "Vegan with a Vengeance"? Such a nice Jewish girl with such anger? (By the way, you will have to read parts of this book in the voice of a Jewish mother—if I had to deal with it, so do you.) Well, not *so* much anger, but like it or not, vegans have something to prove. The image of the emaciated vegan living in depravity on a handful of nuts, grass, and brown rice is tiresome. I want to feed this proverbial vegan. But we have something to prove to each other. It seems that many vegans depend on store-bought processed food. Of course, I indulge in frozen veggie burgers now and then, but that's not the point. The point is that a vegan can go his or her whole life without ever laying a vegetable on a cutting board. I cringe at this notion for several reasons: (1) It is culinarily incorrect. Great cooks depend on fresh ingredients; nothing beats home-made. I am hell-bent on making a great cook out of each and every vegan. (2) It's expensive. One of the benefits of a vegan diet is its affordability. Beans bought in bulk will beat out a package of veggie crumbles every time. (3) It makes us vegans dependent on huge corporations with shady policies. It's nicer to spend our money on locally grown vegetables and small independent businesses wherever possible. Don't worry, those veggie burgers will still be bought by people with heart problems or on diets, and I think that is more their target market anyway. Okay, I've made my point—I promise that the heavy-handedness ends here.

So Who Am I and How Did I Come to Write This Cookbook?

YOU DESERVE TO know. After all, you are about to trust me with your taste buds. A cookbook isn't just light beach reading; it becomes a part of your life. In a few months' time it will be scribbled with your notes and splashed with tamari and tomato sauce. Its food-stained, dog-eared pages will bring back memories of a potluck or the time you spilled an entire bottle of vanilla extract while baking your best friend's birthday cake.

My story begins in Brooklyn, New York. My mother swears up and down that we were a family of domestics, baking cookies and wearing aprons, making light conversation over the cutting board. Passing the salt. I hate to disagree because she's my mother and I love her to pieces, but she taught me a lot of things and cooking wasn't one of them. (If you needed to know how to curse in Yiddish, though, she could help you out.) The fact was I spent most evenings eating dinner at friends' houses. No need to break out the violins; the cool thing about it was that growing up in Brooklyn and mooching off of everyone's parents gave me a wonderful sense of culinary diversity. Italian, Puerto Rican, Jewish, Indian—I got to experience it all and those tastes and flavors are a part of who I am and what I cook now.

The Brooklyn I grew up in wasn't the Brooklyn that we know today—that of lattes and Pilates, converted lofts and jogging strollers. It was more like "drive your IROC-Z, blast your underground disco, and throw McDonald's wrappers out your car window at anyone who dresses a little different or whom you suspect knows how to read." I was often confused and searching for real meaning—I knew that there was more to life then getting into fistfights with other big-haired girls in our crappy mall. So I started going to Manhattan with my best friend. And it wasn't the Manhattan that we know today—that of tenement-turned-luxury apartment and *Sex and the City* wannabes. It was exciting and artistic and "skateboarding is not a crime" and "Whose friggin park? Our friggin park!"

I had been hanging out more and more on the Lower East Side and getting involved with the anarchist scene there. I was not yet sure where my political affinities lay, but I knew that I respected what the activists and punks were doing: taking old decrepit buildings and turning them into homes, creating community gardens, making their own newspapers and zines, and just generally giving a damn. I had already been listening to punk and dying my hair purple and making my own clothes. Vegetarianism was not a new concept to me—at the age of eight I made the horrifying connection that Puff Kit, our cat, was an animal just like the cows we ate. Once I started meeting people who were vegetarian it felt like the most logical and ethical way to be. I already knew that I didn't want to be part of a system of oppression; changing my diet was an easy and practical form of activism.

When I went vegetarian, food seemed to become the focal point of my life—volunteering for Food Not Bombs, cooking breakfast for everyone before a demonstration, making snacks as we silk-screened or made banners. I realized I had a knack for cooking and it was something that I enjoyed and everyone appreciated. I remember the first time I smelled basil fresh from the garden—I almost cried. I was hooked.

The Cinderella Story

FLASH FORWARD TO my thirties. After many culinary adventures—some of which you'll read about in this book—I wrote a cookbook, *this* cookbook in fact. It's quite the Cinderella story, except without all the sexism.

Not too long after September 11, which I had witnessed from my bedroom window, I was somewhat depressed and bored, feeling a bit like I was wasting my life. I was largely disconnected from the punk scene I grew up in; most of my old friends had drifted away. Dividing my time between a cubicle job and cooking at a vegan café, I was also watching a lot of cooking shows on TV. This proved to be a volatile combination—I found myself doing my own cooking show in my head. I couldn't just prepare the BBQ tempeh and greens; I had to walk an imaginary audience through the whole thing.

It was while watching Emeril butcher yet another innocent chicken that I thought, "Someone should really do a vegan cooking show." And then I realized, "I'm someone! I can do it!" If punk rock taught me anything, it's that we can create our own forms of entertainment. We don't have to sit back idly and wait for something to happen—we can make it happen. CRASS lyrics drifted through my head: "If the program's not the one you want, get up turn off the set. It's only you that can decide the life you're gonna get."

And so I took a monthlong class at BCAT (Brooklyn Community Access TV) that taught me the basics of editing, camera work, and lighting. Then I spent weeks agonizing over what to call the show. I thought it had to be something that sounded vaguely punk because punk was the culture I grew up in and the culture that made me the woman I am. But I wasn't feeling that punk anymore—after all, I had a food processor and a job in a cubicle. Fine—Post Punk. *You know*, not so punk anymore. The *Post Punk Kitchen* was born. At the time, I actually didn't realize that "post punk" was a thing unto itself—the music that came after punk—but, oh well, that's not what I meant. I meant it as sort of a self-conscious joke about the people with a punk rock ethos, like me, who are getting older and facing the conundrum of growing up and making compromises that their eighteen-year-old selves might hate them for.

I created a Web site that instantly gained popularity by becoming a Yahoo! pick of the day. They wrote a very flattering review of my TV show. Thing was, I still didn't have a TV show. Shortly after that *Bust* magazine contacted me to do a little piece about the nonexistent show. I was ecstatic. I called my friend and former vegan chef Terry and said, "Hey, want to be in this article with me?" She agreed. I then got her to agree to be the guest host in the first episode, which would feature sushi. Now, Terry is a complete sushi slut and she can't possibly say no to anything that shows off her sushi skills. (Little did she know that I was actually roping her into my cult and that she would never be able to escape.) Then my friend and upstairs neighbor, Denise, who worked in independent media and television production, said she was really excited about the idea of the show. She volunteered her collective production company to handle all the technical aspects.

When we actually started producing the show it seemed to strike a chord with people—two girls cooking in a real kitchen, making stupid sex jokes, and having a punk rock band in the living room chopping vegetables. I got so many wonderful letters over the following year—mothers with children that were lactose intolerant, seasoned vegans and vegetarians who wanted to thank us, people who just loved food and liked the show, new vegetarians with cooking questions. Lots of people asked if we had a cookbook, so I began to look into self-publishing.

Now comes the Cinderella part. Across the country, a big-shot Beverly Hills literary agent, dressed in white, smoking a Cuban cigar with pinky rings on his finger (that is my artistic embellishment; he's actually a mild-mannered Minor Threat fan originally from Ohio) called me and asked if he could pitch my book.

And now you're holding it in your hands. I hope that if you're a new cook, it will empower you to be fearless in the kitchen. I hope that if you are an experienced cook, you will enjoy my take on things. If only one potluck is a success then my job here is done. But there better be a heck of a lot more than one.

I would love to hear from you. Check out *The Post Punk Kitchen* Web site at www.theppk.com.

How to Use This Book

FIZZLE IS MY CAT. He often sits on the counter while I prep things. I know it's unsanitary, but really, there is no keeping him away, so I decided to put him to work in the book since he can't work in real life. (Fizzle doesn't actually know how to cook—he's just a cat.) Throughout the book he offers little tidbits of information that aren't necessarily integral to the recipe, but that you might want to know—like the fact that miso is thought to fight radiation sickness and that flax seeds contain omega-3 fatty acids.

You'll also see Punk Points throughout, little tips that help make cooking or prepping a dish easier, like my top-secret technique for prepping a butternut squash.

Other than that there is nothing mysterious going on—just follow the recipes and use my suggested substitutions if you need to. I remember once reading a Betty Crocker cookbook that asked readers not to deviate from a recipe—well I say no such thing. Deviate all you want, recipes are mere guidelines and everyone has different tastes. If the final dish tastes good to you, then it's a success.

Tools and Kitchen Stuff

I HAVE A love-hate relationship with cooking supply stores. On the one hand, I love looking at all the fancy cookware and appliances, but on the other hand, do I really need brightly enameled French saucepans? No. But of course I go ahead and buy one anyway. That's the problem. To help you avoid the same pitfalls, I've provided a list below of those items I *actually* use.

- ✗ A good knife is so totally necessary. It'll cost you about $100 new, but you only need one and it'll last a lifetime. I recommend an 8-inch chef's knife. Professional knife sharpeners are a dying breed, but if you can find one, have him/her sharpen your knife for you—those sharpeners they sell in stores are crap. Take care of your knife and it will take care of you!

- ✗ I know I said you only need one knife but a serrated knife is mighty handy, too—you can go cheap here, though. Not just for bread; you can cut tomatoes more easily with a serrated blade. Don't use it on onions, though, unless you need a really good cry.

- ✗ A paring knife is also useful. Not so much for paring, but for opening packages, cutting delicate things, etc. So you need three knives, really, a chef's knife, a serrated knife, and a paring knife. But that's it, for real this time.

- ✗ I used to have a wooden cutting board but the damned thing got wet and mildewy on me. Plus it was a pain to clean. Now I have one of those plastic cutting boards with a rubber grip bottom and it's great. It doesn't slide all over the place and I can just throw it in the sink and not worry about mold. Whatever you do, don't use a glass cutting board: they look cool but they'll just destroy your knives.

- ✗ Bowls for mixing! A set of stainless-steel bowls is a nice thing to have; you can drop them and they won't break. Plus they're cheap. I have a big heavy Pyrex bowl that I like to use for bread and hot things, but it's a pain to clean (it doesn't fit in the sink so well) and it's *heavy*. I also have a bajillion little bowls and ramekins that I use but they're totally not necessary.

✗ A big cast-iron frying pan will change your life. It adds great flavor plus iron to food and it gets hot and stays hot. New ones don't cost a lot and you can buy used ones, too—if there's rust on the pan, scrub it off with steel wool and then give the pan a light coating of oil and place it in a hot oven to season it. Never ever wash your cast-iron pans with soap, and don't scrub 'em too hard, either! After a while, cooking oil will coat the pans and bake on, giving them a nonstickish kind of surface that also protects the iron from rust. When this happens the pans will become easy to clean; just soak 'em for a few minutes in hot water and clean them with a brush. Then dry them; if they stay wet they'll rust.

✗ A nonstick skillet is a good thing to have, too, one that won't dent easily and has a solid, well-attached handle. Remember not to use metal utensils with a nonstick surface! If you scratch it, it'll start to flake off and then it's useless; you'll have to throw it out. So take care of it. Don't get it super-hot, either; use a cast-iron skillet for that sort of thing.

✗ A metal spatula (for the cast-iron pan) and a wooden spatula (for the nonstick). I like those cheap metal spatulas with a thin, flexible paddle.

✗ Tongs are your best friend. I use them for flipping things and for grabbing things that are high up on shelves.

✗ It's nice to have smaller pans for smaller things. I use a nonstick pan for toasting spices and melting chocolate. Try to purchase one that you can put in the oven as well (with a handle that won't melt), which is great for frittatas.

✗ For years I had this thrift-store 6-quart pot that I used for everything, but some rice burned into it and it had a broken handle anyway, so I had to throw it out. Now I have a 4-quart pot and a giant 3-gallon pot. I hardly ever use the giant pot but, when I need it, I really need it, so it's great to have.

✗ My sister gave me a cast-iron grill pan that she didn't want, and that thing has revolutionized my life. I don't know how I lived without it. And it's not a terribly expensive item, either, so I don't know why I didn't have one. So awesome.

✗ A big spoon for stirring things and a ladle for soups.

VEGAN WITH VENGEANCE

✗ A box grater for shredding things and a microplane for shaving things, zesting lemons, etc.

✗ A nice peeler, preferably a Y-shaped serrated one for peeling veggies with thick skins.

✗ A whisk, for whisking!

✗ My rubber spatula melted when I left it too close to the stove. So I went and bought one of those silicon ones—problem solved. Great for getting all the batter out of the mixing bowls.

✗ A frying thermometer, not to be confused with a meat thermometer or a candy thermometer. A frying thermometer can measure temperatures up to 500°F (the other thermometers quit a hundred or two degrees lower than that), and should come with a clip or hook to let you hang the gizmo inside the pot.

✗ I buy baking sheets, muffin tins, etc., as I need them. A good rimmed cookie sheet is a must-have. Get a cheap 9 × 13-inch baking pan for roasting—stuff will burn and get stuck in it, so you don't want to use your good one. I really like my Pyrex casserole, and my glass pie plate.

✗ I have a lot of baking accoutrements but the things I use every time I bake are my sifter (which is actually a stainless steel strainer) and my wooden spoon.

✗ You don't want to do without a blender. It's great for whizzing tofu into a puree, or making pesto and other sauces. I use my blender almost daily.

Things That I Have but That Aren't Totally Necessary

✗ A handheld mixer for mixing batter.

✗ A handheld blender for pureeing soups.

✗ A small coffee grinder for grinding spices.

✗ A food processor for chopping, mixing dough, pureeing sauces, and making hummus. It may be too expensive to be essential, but if you get married or can finagle another way to register for gifts, someone might buy you one.

✗ A hammer or mallet for crushing seeds.

The Post Punk Pantry

NOTHING MAKES ME happier than a well-stocked pantry. But of course I always find myself running out of cumin in the middle of cooking up a batch of scrambled tofu, or, halfway through mixing a cake batter I discover that I'm out of vanilla extract. So a well-stocked pantry is more of an ideal than a practical reality. Still, I've compiled this list of what my mythical well-stocked pantry *would* contain, as a guide for you.

Herbs, Spices, and Seasonings

Preground Spices: allspice, anise, black pepper in a pepper mill, cardamom, cayenne, chile powder, Chinese five-spice, cinnamon, cloves, coriander, cumin, curry powder, ginger, nutmeg, paprika, turmeric
Whole Spices: cardamom seeds, cinnamon sticks, cloves, coriander seeds, cumin seeds, fennel seeds, mustard seeds, nutmeg.
Dried Herbs: bay leaves, marjoram, oregano, rosemary, tarragon, thyme.

Grains and Rice

Arborio rice, basmati rice, brown rice, couscous (not technically a grain but still), millet, quinoa.

Dried Beans

Black-eyed peas, black beans, chickpeas (garbanzo beans), French lentils, navy beans, pinto beans, red lentils, split peas.

Nuts (stored in the freezer)

Almonds, cashews, hazelnuts, macadamia nuts, peanuts, pumpkin seeds, walnuts.

Canned Goods

Black beans, chickpeas, coconut milk, pineapple juice, tomato paste, whole tomatoes in juice.

Noodles

Linguine, macaroni, rice noodles, soba noodles.

Baking Stuff

Almond extract, arrowroot, all-purpose flour, baking chocolate (semi-sweet), baking powder, baking soda, chocolate chips, cocoa powder, cornmeal, cornstarch, Dutch-processed cocoa powder, flax seeds (whole or ground), lemon extract, maple extract, pure vanilla extract, raisins, rolled oats, shredded coconut, tapioca starch (also called tapioca flour), whole-wheat pastry flour.

Frozen Fruits and Veggies

Artichoke hearts, corn, edamame, peas, spinach, various berries and fruit.

In the Fridge

Capers, Dijon mustard, extra-firm tofu, peanut butter, rice milk, soy milk, tahini, tempeh, Vegannaise (vegan mayonnaise).

Vinegars, Oils, and Liquid Things

apple cider vinegar, balsamic vinegar, Bragg Liquid Aminos, brown rice syrup, canola oil, olive oil, peanut oil, pure maple syrup, red wine vinegar, rice wine vinegar, soy sauce, white cooking wine.

Other Vegan Must-Haves:

nutritional yeast, textured vegetable protein, vital wheat gluten, extra-firm silken tofu (vacuum-packed).

Brunch is probably my favorite meal in the world. I love waking up to the smell of onions and coffee and pancakes. In reality it's usually me doing the cooking and others waking up to it because I'm generous like that. But for whoever is doing the cooking, try to prep as much as you can the night before so that you can roll out of bed and get things going.

BRUNCH

Scrambled Tofu

I eat scrambled tofu at least three times a week. This is my basic recipe but feel free to add any finely chopped vegetables that you want to use up; add them when you add the mushrooms. Broccoli, zucchini, and cauliflower are all great contenders. The most important thing is that you get the texture right; you want it to be chunky. As you cook the tofu it will crumble more, so just break it into big chunks through your fingers right into the pan. This is a great tasting way to introduce a tofuphobe to the heavenly bean curd we all know and love.

>   1 tablespoon olive oil
>   1 medium-size yellow onion, chopped into ½-inch chunks
>   2 cups thinly sliced cremini mushrooms
>   2 to 3 cloves garlic, minced
>   1 pound extra-firm tofu, drained
>   ¼ cup nutritional yeast
>   Juice of ½ lemon
>   1 carrot, peeled (optional, I grate it in at the end, mostly for color)

>   FOR SPICE BLEND:
>   2 teaspoons ground cumin
>   1 teaspoon dried thyme, crushed with your fingers
>   1 teaspoon ground paprika
>   ½ teaspoon ground turmeric
>   1 teaspoon salt

Heat the oil in a skillet over medium-high heat. Sauté the onions for 3 minutes, until softened; add the mushrooms, sauté for 5 minutes; add the garlic, sauté for 2 minutes. Add the spice blend and mix it up for 15 seconds or so. Add ¼ cup water to deglaze the pan, scraping the bottom to get all the garlic and spices.

Crumble in the tofu and mix well. Don't crush the tofu, just kind of lift it and mix it around. You want it to remain chunky. Let cook for about 15 minutes, stirring occasionally and adding splashes of water if necessary to keep it from sticking too much. Lower the heat a bit if you find that the tofu is sticking. Add the lemon juice. Add the nutritional yeast and mix it up. If the mixture is sticking to the pan, add splashes of water. The moistness really depends on how much water the tofu was retaining before you added it.

Grate the carrot into the tofu mixture and fold. Serve with guacamole and salsa and potatoes and toast and tempeh bacon.

VEGAN WITH A VENGEANCE

VARIATIONS

Tofu Rancheros: Add 1 cup of Salsa at the end, cook for 1 minute extra.

Asian-Style Scrambled Tofu: Add 2 tablespoons of minced ginger with the garlic, use peanut oil instead of olive oil, substitute shiitake mushrooms, and omit the thyme and nutritional yeast. Mix in 1 cup of thinly sliced scallions at the very end.

PUNK POINTS

If you don't have nutritional yeast on hand you can still make this recipe; just don't add any water when cooking.

Fizzle says:

Use a cast-iron pan so that you don't have to worry about scratching the pan to get all the good burnt bits.

VEGAN WITH A VENGEANCE

Asparagus and Sun-dried Tomato Frittata

A frittata is an open-faced, baked omelet. I love the combo of asparagus and sun-dried tomatoes for its colors as well as taste and texture, but you can get creative with your vegetable choices or use some of my variations below. No need to press the tofu, just drain it and give it a squeeze over the sink—that oughta do it.

1 pound extra-firm tofu

1 tablespoon soy sauce

1 teaspoon Dijon mustard (yellow will work fine if you like that better)

¼ cup nutritional yeast

2 teaspoons olive oil

½ cup onion (1 small), cut into ¼-inch dice

3 stalks asparagus, rough ends discarded, cut into bite-size pieces

¼ cup sun-dried tomatoes packed in oil, finely chopped

2 cloves garlic, minced

1 teaspoon dried thyme

¼ teaspoon ground turmeric

Juice of ½ lemon

¼ cup fresh basil leaves, torn into pieces

Preheat oven to 400°F.

In a mixing bowl, crumble the tofu and squeeze through your fingers until it resembles ricotta cheese. This should take about a minute. Mix in the soy sauce and mustard. Add the nutritional yeast and combine well. Set aside.

In a small (8-inch) skillet, sauté the onions in the olive oil for 2 minutes. Add asparagus and sun-dried tomatoes, sauté for about 3 more minutes. Add the garlic and thyme and turmeric, sauté for 1 more minute. Add the lemon juice to deglaze the pan; turn off the heat. Transfer the onion mixture to the tofu mixture and combine well. Fold in the basil leaves. Transfer back to the skillet and press the mixture firmly in place. Cook in the oven at 400°F for 20 minutes. Transfer to the broiler to brown the top, about 2 minutes (keep a close eye on it so as not to burn it). Let the frittata sit for 10 minutes before serving. Cut into four slices and lift each piece out with a pie server to prevent the frittata from falling apart. If it does crumble a bit, don't fret, just put it back into shape.

VARIATIONS

Broccoli and Olive Frittata: Replace the asparagus with ½ cup chopped broccoli florettes. Replace the sundried-tomatoes with sliced black olives.

Indian Frittata: Replace the asparagus with ½ cup chopped cauliflower florettes. Replace the sun-dried tomatoes with ¼ cup cooked chickpeas. Omit the thyme and basil, add 1 teaspoon curry powder and one teaspoon cumin.

Mushroom Frittata: Saute 1 cup of sliced cremini mushrooms along with the onions. Omit the asparagus, use ¼ cup of sliced black olives or sun-dried tomatoes. Serve with Mushroom Sauce (page 89).

PUNK POINTS

If you don't have an 8-inch skillet then employ a pie plate when baking the fritatta.

VEGAN WITH A VENGEANCE

As a vegan, the hardest part about not eating eggs is going out with friends for brunch. That is one of the only times I feel resentment toward my omnivore associates: when I am sitting in a diner as they enjoy waffles and omelets and I have to make do with a bowl of oatmeal. But you can take the matter into your own hands and start your own brunch café—it's more fun and more social than having a hungover waiter spill coffee on you at a $13.00 prix fixe.

First, you need to decide on a space. When I lived in a loft this was easy—we had a huge open space available to us and we were able to pack the place with as many as fifty people on any given Sunday. But if you have a smaller space to work with, clear everything out of the biggest room, throw some pillows on the floor, or get a huge communal table. I've hosted cafés at bookstores and even in a church basement—you don't even need a stove if you have a toaster oven and a hot plate, and invest in a few Sterno-heated portable serving trays.

For the food, the easiest thing to do is prepare dishes that are easy to cook in large quantities and keep warm. Here is my typical menu:

Breakfast Burritos

Cook a huge batch of scrambled tofu. Keep it warm on the stovetop over very low heat, stirring whenever you get a chance. Prepare a lot of guacamole and fresh salsa. Shred a few blocks of soy cheese beforehand (totally optional, the burritos are just as good without it). Buy flour tortillas and roll the tofu and cheese into a burrito, with a dollop of guac and salsa on top.

Herb-Roasted Potatoes (page 25)

These keep well all day, either in a 200°F oven or in a serving tray. Serve with the breakfast burritos.

Tempeh Bacon (page 23)

Keep warm in a serving tray or in a 200°F oven.

Waffles

Make all the waffles the night before and refrigerate. You'll just need to reheat them in the toaster the next day; sometimes they taste even better than fresh waffles because they get crispier when they are toasted. Serve with sliced strawberries and bananas and maple syrup.

Tofu, Potatoes, and Tempeh

Make another dish out of the scrambled tofu with roasted potatoes and tempeh, serve with a tortilla or toast.

Have a huge pot of coffee freshly brewed at all times. You can employ a Thermos for the coffee and set up a coffee-serving station with the sugar and soy creamer so guests can fix their own.

When I used to throw brunch cafés, we'd usually charge five dollars a person, which always covered costs and even netted a couple of extra dollars to invest in the next café. The point obviously isn't to make money, but to have a good time. We sometimes got a DJ to spin hip-hop, punk, and '80s music, so it was really more of a party during the day. I definitely suggest playing some music, whatever you like, and if you have some board games and cards, they'll make things even more (nerdy) fun.

VEGAN WITH VENGEANCE

Tempeh and White Bean Sausage Patties

I love the combination of white beans and tempeh. The beans have a naturally smoky flavor, and the tempeh and herbs give these patties the savory taste I crave upon rolling out of bed on a Sunday morning or (let's be honest) afternoon. They have a softer texture than store-bought vegetarian sausage patties, but a much better flavor. You can prepare the mix up to two days in advance so that all you have to do the day of serving is form the patties and cook.

1 pound tempeh, crumbled into bite-size pieces
4 teaspoons Bragg Liquid Aminos or tamari (or soy sauce for that matter)
1 cup cooked white beans
3 tablespoons olive oil
2 cloves garlic, minced
1 teaspoon fennel seed, crushed
1 heaping tablespoon chopped fresh thyme
1 heaping teaspoon chopped fresh sage, (about 5 leaves)
Pinch of ground cayenne pepper
Pinch of ground nutmeg
1 tablespoon tomato paste
¼ cup plain bread crumbs
Dash of salt
A few dashes fresh black pepper

Place the tempeh into a saucepan and just barely cover with water (it's okay, even preferable, if some of the tempeh is peeking out of the water). Add 1 teaspoon of Bragg, cover and bring to a boil. Simmer for about 15 minutes, or until most of the water is absorbed. Drain any remaining water and transfer the tempeh to a large bowl. Add the white beans, give a quick stir, and set aside. This will heat the beans just a bit for easier mashing and cool the tempeh down just a bit for easier handling.

Give the saucepan a quick rinse and dry. Sauté the garlic and fennel seed in 1 tablespoon olive oil over low heat, just until fragrant (about 1 minute). Add the remainder of the spices and stir constantly for 30 seconds. Add to the tempeh mixture along with the tomato paste and remaining tablespoon of Bragg.

Mash everything together with a potato masher or strong fork, until it's just a bit chunky and there are no whole beans left (you don't want it pureed, you should still be able to see the beans). Add the bread crumbs and combine well with a fork. Taste for salt and spices and adjust to your liking. Let sit for about 15 minutes to allow the flavors to meld.

Form into patties, using about 3 tablespoons' worth of the mix (you can use a quarter-cup measuring cup filled three-quarters full to make the patties consistent in size). Heat the remaining 2 tablespoons of olive oil over medium heat. Cook the patties until brown, about 3 minutes each side. You may need to add a little more oil when you flip them over.

VEGAN WITH A
VENGEANCE

Breakfast Veggie Chorizo

I often enjoy this delicious dish with a breakfast burrito; however, it makes a great accompaniment to any meal with Latin flair. Ancho chile powder tastes best here but if you can't find it and don't feel like making your own, you can substitute regular chile powder.

2 tablespoons olive oil

1 medium-size onion, very finely chopped

3 cloves garlic, minced

1 teaspoon salt

2 teaspoons coriander seed, crushed

2 teaspoons cumin seed, crushed

½ teaspoon fennel seed, crushed

2 tablespoons ancho chile powder

1 teaspoon dried oregano

1 tablespoon sugar

3 cups water

1 cup Textured Vegetable Protein (TVP)

2 bay leaves

1 cinnamon stick

3 tablespoons tomato paste

A very healthy dose freshly ground black pepper

 *Fizzle says:*

Textured Vegetable Protein, often called TVP, is soy beans that have been defatted, pressure cooked, and dried, leaving only the protein. The end product is sold in small dry chunks, usually in the bulk section at the health food store. Once rehydrated and cooked, TVP has a chewy, meaty texture. It comes in small or large chunks. We prefer to use the small chunks but the large ones will work as well.

Preheat a medium-size saucepan for a minute or so, add the oil and onions and sauté for 3 minutes. Add the garlic and sauté for another 30 seconds; add the salt, spices, and sugar; sauté for another 2 minutes. Add the water, TVP, bay leaves, cinnamon stick, and tomato paste, cover and bring to a boil. Lower heat and simmer for 10 more minutes. Uncover and remove the cinnamon stick; cook for 5 minutes more, uncovered, until most of the water has been absorbed and reduced. Add freshly ground pepper to taste. You can serve immediately but I prefer to cover and let sit for 20 or so minutes to let the TVP absorb all the flavors.

PUNK POINTS

To quickly crush the seeds, place them in a coffee grinder and pulse three or four times. If you are too punk for a coffee grinder, place the seeds in a plastic bag and cover with a thin towel or even a few pieces of newspaper, and proceed to hammer with a mallet or a regular hammer, until the neighbors complain.

VEGAN WITH A VENGEANCE

Tempeh Sausage Crumbles

When I first began writing this book I wasn't sure what section to put this recipe into because I use it in so many different kinds of meals—in pasta sauce, in gravy, as a side dish for brunch. I decided to put it here, but don't be afraid to experiment with it.

1 (8-ounce) package tempeh
1 tablespoon fennel seed
1 teaspoon dried basil
1 teaspoon dried marjoram or oregano
½ teaspoon red pepper flakes
½ teaspoon dried sage
2 cloves garlic, minced
2 tablespoons tamari or soy sauce
1 tablespoon olive oil
Juice of ½ lemon

In a small pan, crumble the tempeh and add enough water to almost cover it. Over medium-high heat, simmer the tempeh until most of the water is absorbed, about 12–15 minutes. Drain the remaining water and add the rest of the ingredients and cook over medium heat, stirring occasionally, until lightly browned, about 10 minutes.

VEGAN WITH A
VENGEANCE

Tempeh Bacon

I love these smoky strips alongside pancakes, or in a BLT or in a salad or in a house or with a mouse. They aren't going to fool any meat eaters, but they'll fully satisfy us herbivores. You need to marinate the tempeh for a good hour so plan ahead or marinate it overnight. Peanut oil adds a richer flavor so I recommend using it, but canola or vegetable oil will do nicely. You can use thinly sliced, pressed tofu if you haven't got any tempeh.

> 3 tablespoons Bragg Liquid Aminos or tamari or soy sauce
> ⅓ cup apple cider
> 1 teaspoon tomato paste
> ¼ teaspoon liquid smoke
> 1 (8-ounce) package tempeh
> 2 cloves garlic, crushed
> 2 tablespoons peanut oil or vegetable oil

To make the marinade, combine the Bragg, cider, tomato paste, and liquid smoke in a wide, shallow bowl and mix with a fork until the tomato paste is fully dissolved. Set aside.

Cut the tempeh into thin strips (less than ¼ inch thick) lengthwise. You should be able to get about twelve strips. Rub the strips with the crushed garlic, then toss the garlic cloves into the marinade. Submerge the tempeh strips in the marinade and let sit, turning occasionally, for at least an hour and up to overnight. After marinating, discard the garlic.

Heat the peanut oil in a large skillet over medium heat. Add the tempeh strips and cook for 4 minutes on one side; the bottom should be nicely browned. Flip the strips over and pour the remainder of the marinade over them; if there isn't much marinade left add a splash of water. Cover and let cook for 3 more minutes, until the liquid is absorbed. Uncover and check for doneness; if necessary, keep cooking uncovered until all sides are nicely browned. Remove from heat and serve.

Sweet Potato Hash with Five-Spice and Watercress

I whipped this up one morning to go with my scrambled tofu when the only vegetables I had around were sweet potatoes and watercress. The watercress made me think Chinese, and the Chinese made me think five-spice powder and thus this simple but delicious creation was born. The watercress does a great job of picking up the spices and the garlic.

> 3 tablespoons olive oil
> 1 medium-size onion, cut into ¼-inch dice
> 2 cloves garlic, minced
> ¼ teaspoon salt
> 1½ teaspoons Chinese five-spice powder
> 3 medium-size sweet potatoes, cut into ½-inch dice
> 1 bunch watercress, stems discarded, torn into big pieces

In a large skillet over medium-high heat, cook the onion in 1 tablespoon of the olive oil for 2 minutes, stirring occasionally. Add the garlic, salt, and five-spice and cook for about 1 minute. Add the sweet potatoes and the rest of the oil. Cook for about 12 to 15 minutes, until the potatoes are cooked and caramelized a bit. Add the watercress and cook, stirring constantly, for 2 more minutes.

Fizzle says:

Chinese five-spice powder incorporates the five basic tastes of Chinese cooking—sweet, sour, bitter, umami (pungent), and salty. The blend commonly sold in America consists of cinnamon, black pepper, cloves, fennel seed, and star anise.

Herb-Roasted Potatoes

You can't have brunch without potatoes—I'd like to see you try. I love these crispy, salty spuds and they are all kinds of easy to prepare. If the small red potatoes are radically different sizes, then cut the larger ones into thirds. They should be approximately 1¼ inches across.

3 pounds small red potatoes, halved widthwise
1 medium-size onion, quartered and sliced ½ inch thick
¼ cup olive oil
2 teaspoons coarse sea salt
Several dashes fresh black pepper
4 teaspoons rosemary, chopped
4 teaspoons chopped fresh thyme

Preheat oven to 450°F. Divide the potatoes and onions between two rimmed baking pans or a large rimmed baking sheet, sprinkle with oil and then salt and pepper, and toss to coat (I find it's easiest to use your hands for this). Roast for 35 minutes. Remove from oven, sprinkle with the herbs, toss to coat (use a spatula now, they're hot! I'm sure you realize this but just in case . . .). Return to oven and roast until brown and tender, about 20 minutes longer.

VEGAN WITH A VENGEANCE

Baking Powder Biscuits and White Bean Tempeh Sausage Gravy

This biscuit recipe is adapted from a 1944 cookbook entitled Ruth Wakefield's Toll House Tried and True Recipes. In her introduction she states, "I know there are no substitutions for butter, cream, eggs, fresh fruits and vegetables for preparing a fine meal." I agree with the fruit and veggies part but aside from that I have thoroughly ignored Ruth's advice, and her modified biscuit recipe has served me well for years. If you'd like, you can serve these with the White Bean Sausage Gravy (recipe follows), the Mushroom Sauce on page 89 or ignore my suggestions as I did Ruth's and serve them with margarine or whatever else you want. The gravy is a modified version of a recipe submitted to my Web site by someone named Lisa. Thanks, Lisa.

> 2 cups all-purpose flour
> 5 teaspoons baking powder
> 1 teaspoons salt
> 3 tablespoons nonhydrogenated shortening
> 2 tablespoons nonhydrogenated margarine
> ⅔ cup rice or soy milk

Preheat oven to 450°F. Lightly grease a cookie sheet.

Sift together the flour, baking powder, and salt. Cut the shortening and margarine into the flour with a pastry knife or your fingers. Add the rice milk to form a soft dough. Mix well and pat out on a floured countertop until about ½ inch thick; cut out 2-inch rounds with the rim of a glass or cookie cutter. Place on prepared cookie sheet and bake for 12 to 15 minutes.

VEGAN WITH A VENGEANCE

White Bean and Tempeh Sausage Gravy

Tempeh Sausage Crumbles (page 22)
2 cups cooked white beans (or one 15-ounce can, drained and rinsed)
2 tablespoons olive oil or margarine, softened
¼ cup vegetable broth or water
½ teaspoon salt
A few dashes fresh black pepper
10 to 12 leaves fresh sage, chopped

Prepare the Tempeh Sausage Crumbles and keep them warm in the pan.

Puree the white beans with the olive oil and vegetable broth in a blender or food processor until relatively smooth. Add to the tempeh crumbles along with the salt and pepper. Heat through for a few minutes. If you want to make the gravy thinner, add a little more vegetable broth. Mix in the sage and cook for another 2 minutes.

"Fronch" Toast

I couldn't tell you what it is about chickpea flour but this French toast looks and tastes just like the "real" thing. Chickpea flour is quite easy to find these days—if you don't have a Middle Eastern grocery store nearby, try a health food store or one of those "gourmet" markets. I like to use a nice crusty baguette for this recipe, but if you want to use sliced bread, make sure to lightly toast it first (see below). Serve with fresh berries, sliced bananas, and pure maple syrup.

Loaf of Italian or French bread, baguette shaped, preferably stale
½ cup soy creamer (rice or soy milk would make a good substitution, preferably rice)
½ cup rice milk or plain soy milk
2 tablespoons cornstarch
¼ cup chickpea flour
Several tablespoons canola or vegetable oil

Slice the bread into 1-inch rounds. The bread should be a bit stale; if not, leave the slices out overnight or put them in a 350°F oven for 3 to 4 minutes to dry them out—you don't want to toast them. (If you're in a rush, feel free to skip this step—the French toast will still taste good.)

Pour the soy creamer and rice milk into a wide, shallow bowl. Mix in the cornstarch and stir until dissolved. Add the chickpea flour and mix until it is mostly absorbed; some lumps are okay.

Heat a nonstick skillet over medium-high heat. Add enough oil to create a thin layer on the bottom (a tablespoon or two).

Soak the bread slices (as many as will fit into your pan) in the mixture and transfer to the skillet. Cook each side for about 2 minutes; if they are not brown enough when you flip them, heat for 1 or 2 more minutes on each side. They should be golden brown with flecks of dark brown. Serve immediately.

*T*here is nothing like a stack of pancakes dripping with maple syrup, served with some smoky tempeh bacon on the side. Although pancake ingredients are fairly simple, the combination of flour and water seems to have an uncanny ability to stress a person out. I'm no motivational speaker, but trust me—it may take a couple of tries to get perfect pancakes but you can do it. Here are some tips to guide you along the way. (If it helps, picture my head in a dream cloud floating above your left shoulder, guiding you on. If that doesn't help and only serves to freak you out, then just follow these guidelines.)

✗ The amount of water you need depends on several factors including altitude and the humidity in the air on any given day. I suggest using the liquid quantities I give as a guideline. First, add ¾ cup of water. If the batter looks too thick, or if your first pancake doesn't bubble up, add the remaining liquid.

✗ Don't overmix the batter. You want a couple of lumps in the flour; overmixed batter results in rubbery pancakes.

✗ You may notice that pancakes get lighter and fluffier as you get to the end of the batter. That's because the gluten in the flour has had some time to relax. Let your pancake batter sit for 10 minutes or so before proceeding. You can even let it sit overnight, covered and refrigerated. If the batter thickens too much, just add a little water to reconstitute it.

✗ Use a heavy-bottomed nonstick skillet for even cooking. Or, you can use a cast-iron pan because it's naturally nonstick.

✗ Make sure the pan is hot enough, but not smoking. Preheat the pan for 2 minutes and that should do the trick. If you flick a couple of drops of water into the pan, the drops should bounce. You can also do a test with a tablespoon or two of batter.

✗ Don't go crazy with the grease. A very thin coating of oil will do it. Use a spray bottle of canola oil for an even coating. Apply a fresh coat every time you start a new batch.

✗ To form your pancakes into perfect circles, use the same amount of batter in a ladle every time. Pour the batter out with a slightly circular motion so that it spreads evenly. Don't just plop it down or the middle will be thicker than the edges. You can also try using a meat baster; just fill it up and squeeze the pancake batter out. You'll be amazed at the perfect circles this creates.

✗ The most important thing is that you don't give up. Some say the first pancake is always a flop, so just keep trying. You will get the hang of it!

Pancakes

Straight up pancakes, just like at the diner at 2:00 AM.

> 1¼ cup all-purpose flour
> 2 teaspoon baking powder
> ½ teaspoon salt
> 1 teaspoon ground cinnamon (optional)
> 2 tablespoons canola oil (any mild tasting vegetable oil will do) plus oil for the pan
> ⅓ cup water
> 1 to 1¼ cups plain rice or soy milk
> 1 teaspoon vanilla extract
> 2 tablespoons pure maple syrup

Oil a large skillet and preheat over medium-high heat about 2 minutes (see Perfect Pancakes sidebar).

Sift together the flour, baking powder, and salt, and cinnamon, if using. In a separate bowl, combine all the other ingredients. Adding wet ingredients to dry, mix until just combined. Do not overmix or the pancakes will be tough; a couple of lumps are okay.

Cook pancakes until browned on the bottom and bubbles form on top, about 4 minutes. Turn the pancakes over and cook until the bottoms are browned and the pancakes are barely firm to touch. Transfer to individual plates. Repeat with remaining batter, adding more oil to the pan as needed.

VARIATIONS

Raspberry Lime: Fold in 1 cup of fresh raspberries and 1 tablespoon of finely grated lime zest.

Blueberry: Fold in 1 cup of fresh blueberries.

VEGAN WITH A VENGEANCE

Coconut Pancakes with Pineapple Sauce

Coconut and nutmeg are a great combination. To transform your kitchen into a tropical paradise, serve these pancakes with pineapple sauce (recipe follows) which is ridiculously easy to make.

- 1¼ cups all-purpose flour
- 2 teaspoons baking powder
- ½ teaspoon salt
- 1 teaspoon ground or freshly grated nutmeg (if using fresh, it's one-third of a whole nutmeg)
- ⅓ cup water
- 1 to 1¼ cups plain rice or soy milk
- 2 tablespoons pure maple syrup
- 1 teaspoon vanilla extract, or use coconut extract if you have it on hand
- 2 tablespoons canola oil (any mild tasting vegetable oil will do), plus oil for the pan
- 1 cup unsweetened shredded coconut

Oil a large skillet and preheat over medium-high heat about 2 minutes (see Perfect Pancakes sidebar).

Sift together the flour, baking powder, salt, and nutmeg. Create a well in the center of the dry ingredients; add the water, rice milk, maple syrup, vanilla, and oil. Mix until just combined, fold in coconut.

If making large pancakes, use a ladle to pour the batter into the pan; most standard ladles will yield a 6-inch pancake. For smaller pancakes, drop batter by ¼ cupfuls into the pan. Cook until bubbles form on top, about 3 minutes. Turn pancakes over and cook until the bottoms are browned and the pancakes are cooked through, about 2 more minutes. Serve immediately or keep warm on a plate covered with foil while you cook the others. Repeat with remaining batter. Serve with pineapple sauce.

VEGAN WITH A VENGEANCE

Pineapple Sauce

MAKES 2 CUPS

1 (20-ounce) can pineapple chunks in juice
2 tablespoons arrowroot powder
3 tablespoons sugar
1 teaspoon vanilla extract

In a saucepan, off the heat, stir the pineapple and juice with the arrowroot until it is mostly dissolved; stir in the sugar. Over medium heat, heat the pan until the sauce thickens, stirring often (about 7 minutes).

VEGAN WITH A
VENGEANCE

Banana-Pecan Pancakes

I called these Banana-Pecan Pancakes just to get your attention; the truth is you can use any nut you like, or even chocolate chips instead. Banana provides great flavor, and of course also makes for a wonderful, fluffy pancake. I made a vow not to use the word "crowd-pleaser" in this cookbook but I am going to sell out and tell you—these are a great crowd-pleaser! Everyone loves them. These cook up thicker than the other pancake recipes so I recommend making smaller pancakes and cooking them three to a pan.

> 1½ cups all-purpose flour
> 1½ teaspoons baking powder
> ½ teaspoon baking soda
> ¼ teaspoon salt
> ⅛ teaspoon ground cinnamon
> 1¼ cups very well-mashed banana
> 1½ cups soy milk plus 1 teaspoon vinegar (let sit for 5 minutes)
> 1 tablespoon canola oil
> 1 teaspoon vanilla extract
> ½ cup pecans, chopped
> Canola oil or cooking spray for the pan

Sift together the flour, baking powder, baking soda, salt, and cinnamon.

In a separate bowl, mix the mashed banana with the soy milk, oil, and vanilla until pretty smooth. Pour the wet ingredients into the dry and mix but do not overmix. Fold in the pecans.

Brush a large nonstick skillet with canola oil or spray with cooking spray and heat over medium-high heat until hot but not smoking. Working in batches of three, pour ¼ cup of batter per pancake into the hot skillet and cook until bubbles appear on the surface and the undersides are golden brown, 1 to 2 minutes. Flip the pancakes with a spatula and cook until golden brown and cooked through, 1 to 2 minutes more. Transfer to a large plate and loosely cover with foil to keep warm, then make more pancakes, brushing or spraying the skillet with oil for each batch.

Serve with sliced bananas and maple syrup.

Chocolate-Chocolate Chip Pancakes

I know. Chocolate for breakfast. Reserve this one for special occasions like Valentine's Day, or don't, just go ahead and be decadent. Serve with Strawberry Sauce (page 240) or fresh raspberries and maple syrup.

> 1 cup plus 2 tablespoons all-purpose flour
> 3 tablespoons cocoa powder
> 2 teaspoons baking powder
> ½ teaspoon salt
> ⅓ cup water
> 1 to 1¼ cups rice or soy milk
> 2 tablespoons canola oil
> 3 tablespoons pure maple syrup
> 1 teaspoon vanilla extract
> ½ teaspoon almond extract (optional)
> ⅓ cup semisweet chocolate chips
> Canola oil or cooking spray for pan

In a large mixing bowl sift together the flour, cocoa powder, baking powder, and salt. Create a well in the center of the flour mixture and add the water, rice milk, oil, maple syrup, and extracts. Mix until just combined, fold in chocolate chips.

Oil and preheat a large skillet over medium-high heat for about 2 minutes.

If making large pancakes, use a ladle to pour the batter into the pan; most standard ladles will yield a 6-inch pancake. For smaller pancakes, drop batter by ¼ cupfuls into pan. Cook until bubbles form on top, about 3 minutes. Turn pancakes over and cook until bottoms are browned and the pancakes are cooked through, about 2 more minutes. Serve immediately or keep warm on a plate covered with foil while you cook the others. Repeat with remaining batter.

VEGAN WITH VENGEANCE

I wouldn't call my mother a saint, but she certainly put up with quite a bit during my adolescence. When my sister and I reached our mid-teens we took to hanging out on the Lower East Side (LES) rather than on Sheepshead Bay, where we lived, because we grew tired of the comments and stuff people threw at us from their car windows.

The LES was a safe place, where we could wander the streets 'til the sun came up. We met people from all over who had traveled to New York to fight in the revolution of the time—fixing up and building the squats, keeping the police at bay, and trying to lay claim to a place of their own. Sometimes we brought the LES back with us to Sheepshead Bay, either because there was a demonstration coming up and we needed to paint banners in the basement or because we managed to bring the punks out to Brighton Beach for a late night party and dip in the water.

In the morning, my mom would awake to a dozen or so strange people scattered about, some in the living room, some making breakfast in the kitchen. "Mom," I would say, "This is Larry, this is Vegan Mike, this is Happy Mike, this is Dirtbag Mike." She'd politely smile and then ask to see me in her room, where she'd promptly slam the door and yell:

"Dirtbag Mike! I have to wake up to Dirtbag Mike?!" (While she had closed the door for privacy, you know the punks were cringing as her voice ripped through the house.)

"Well, yes, but there's also Happy Mike." (Did she have a problem looking at the bright side?)

Expletives would follow. Scrambled tofu was left to burn as my mom geared into the business of throwing everyone out. Usually not everyone left. The wise ones knew that if they waited out the storm, the sun would come out and my mom would either cook us all tofu balls and spaghetti or order cheeseless pizza for the brave stragglers who remained. Such was life in Sheepshead Bay in the late '80s. We didn't know at the time that we were ushering in a new age when our lip rings would become not only fashionable but, eventually, passé. It was simultaneously gratifying and horrifying to go back to the old neighborhood in the '90s and see those same guys who once threw a McDonald's Shamrock Shake at me years ago now sporting blue Mohawks. I suppose I could truly measure progress if now they threw a block of tofu at me instead. I'm still waiting.

Ginger-Pear Waffles

When grating the pear for these waffles, leave the skin on—it adds a nice texture and interesting flecks of color. It's best if you choose a pear that is a little underripe, which makes the grating easier and gives off less moisture. If you want to add even more gingery goodness, fold in a tablespoon of finely chopped crystallized ginger.

2 cups all-purpose flour
2 teaspoons baking powder
1 teaspoon baking soda
½ teaspoon salt
2 teaspoons ground ginger
½ teaspoon ground cinnamon
¼ teaspoon ground allspice
¼ teaspoon ground or freshly grated nutmeg
1 cup pear or apple juice
¾ cup soy milk
⅓ cup applesauce
2 tablespoons corn oil (canola or vegetable oil will do)
4 tablespoons sugar
2 teaspoons vanilla extract
1 Bosc pear, grated

Preheat waffle iron according to the manufacturer's directions.

Sift together the flour, baking powder, baking soda, salt, and spices in a large mixing bowl. In a medium-size bowl, mix together the juice, soy milk, applesauce, oil, sugar, and vanilla until well combined. Create a well in the center of the flour mixture and slowly blend the wet ingredients into the dry until combined. Fold in the grated pear.

Make your waffles according to the manufacturer's directions. I use a Belgian waffle iron, and 1 cup of batter per waffle works for me. For crispier waffles, let cook 30 seconds to a minute longer than the directions suggest.

VEGAN WITH VENGEANCE

Oatmeal-Banana-Raisin Waffles

I love the texture the oatmeal gives these waffles. They are chewy and have a hint of banana and cinnamon, with sweet bursts of raisins.

1 cup plus 2 tablespoons all-purpose flour
2 teaspoons baking powder
1 teaspoon baking soda
1¼ teaspoons ground cinnamon
¼ teaspoon ground nutmeg
½ teaspoon salt
1 cup quick-cooking (rolled) oats
1 very ripe medium-size banana
1½ cups soy milk
3 tablespoons pure maple syrup
3 tablespoons vegetable oil
¾ cup raisins
Extra sliced bananas for the top

Preheat waffle iron according to the manufacturer's directions.

In a mixing bowl sift together the flour, baking powder, baking soda, cinnamon, nutmeg, and salt. Add the oatmeal and toss together.

In a separate bowl mash the banana very well. Add the soy milk, maple syrup, and vegetable oil. I use a handheld blender to blend everything together; if you don't have one mix vigorously with a strong fork until there are very few clumps of banana left. Add the wet ingredients to the dry and mix just until combined. Fold in the raisins. Let the batter sit for 2 minutes before making the waffles; this allows the oatmeal to get moist and blend with the rest of the batter.

Prepare the waffles according to the manufacturer's directions. Serve with margarine, maple syrup, and sliced bananas on top.

Lemon Corn Waffles with Blueberry Sauce

Lemon + corn = heaven. Lemon + corn + blueberries = the VIP section of heaven. You can even up the ante by drizzling a little Macadamia Crème (page 240) over the Blueberry Sauce (recipe follows).

1¼ cups plus 2 tablespoons all-purpose flour
2 teaspoons baking powder
1 teaspoon baking soda
½ teaspoon salt
¾ cup cornmeal
¼ cup corn oil (vegetable or canola oil will do)
2 cups soy milk
¼ cup soy yogurt
Zest and juice from 2 lemons
¼ cup sugar

Preheat waffle iron according to the manufacturer's directions.

Sift together the flour, baking powder, baking soda, salt, and cornmeal in a large mixing bowl. In a medium-size bowl, mix together the oil, soy milk, soy yogurt, lemon juice, and sugar until well combined. Create a well in the center of the flour mixture and mix in the wet ingredients just until combined. Make your waffles according to the manufacturer's directions.

Blueberry Sauce

1½ tablespoons arrowroot powder
1 pound frozen blueberries, partially thawed
½ cup maple syrup
1 teaspoon vanilla extract

In a small saucepan off the heat, toss the arrowroot with the blueberries until it is mostly dissolved. This takes about 5 minutes; mix occasionally.

Over medium heat, cook until moisture is released and blueberries are warm. Add the maple syrup and vanilla; heat 5 more minutes, until the sauce thickens a bit.

VEGAN WITH VENGEANCE

Pumpkin Waffles

I used to serve these at Sunday brunch at the doghouse, a loft in Brooklyn I once lived in. It was so great to smell these cooking on those freezing cold winter mornings. Yeah, we had no heat, but we compensated with the best vegan waffles you've ever tasted. Serve these with maple syrup and tempeh bacon. This recipe makes a lot of waffles, so feel free to halve it.

2½ cups all-purpose flour
2½ teaspoons baking powder
½ teaspoon baking soda
½ teaspoon salt
2 teaspoons ground cinnamon
1 teaspoon ground ginger
½ teaspoon ground or freshly grated nutmeg
¼ teaspoon ground cloves
2 cups rice or soy milk
1 (15-ounce) can pureed pumpkin (not pumpkin pie mix)
⅓ cup oil
⅓ cup brown sugar
2 teaspoons vanilla extract

Preheat waffle iron according to the manufacturer's instructions.

Sift together the flour, baking powder, baking soda, salt, and spices. In a separate bowl, vigorously whisk together the soy milk, pumpkin, oil, brown sugar, and vanilla until well emulsified. Pour the wet ingredients into the dry and mix. Prepare the waffles according to the manufacturer's instructions.

VEGAN WITH A VENGEANCE

Whenever I bake muffins I can't help but sing the Black Flag song "Rise Above." Then I get really vegan cheesy and change the lyrics around: "We are born with muffin pans! (Rise Above!) I am gonna have my pan (Rise Above!)." I can't believe I just told the world this but try these delicious muffins and scones and that will help me save some face.

MUFFINS AND SCONES

Scones

Scones are not just flat muffins, as some cafés would have you believe, they're more like doughy biscuits. This is my basic recipe, but I often make the variations listed below.

> 3 cups all-purpose flour
> 2 tablespoons baking powder
> ¼ cup sugar, plus an extra teaspoon for sprinkling the tops
> ¼ teaspoon salt
> ⅓ cup vegetable oil
> ½ cup soy cream (rice or soy milk makes a fine substitution)
> ¾ cup rice or soy milk plus 2 teaspoons apple cider vinegar

Preheat oven to 400°F. Lightly grease a cookie sheet.

In a large mixing bowl, sift together the flour, baking powder, sugar, and salt. Add the oil, soy cream, and rice milk. Mix until just combined; the dough should be clumpy and not sticky. Even if there is still a light dusting of flour, that's okay.

Drop by ¼ cupfuls onto the greased cookie sheet and pat the tops just a bit to round them out; sprinkle with a bit of sugar. Bake 12 to 15 minutes, until slightly browned on the bottom and firm on the top.

VARIATIONS

Berry Scones: Fold in 1½ cups of fresh berries.

Chocolate Chip Scones: Add 1 teaspoon of vanilla extract to the liquid ingredients, add 2 tablespoons of sugar, fold in 1 cup of chocolate chips.

Maple Walnut: Add 2 teaspoons of maple extract to the liquid ingredients, add 2 tablespoons of sugar, fold in 1½ cups of walnuts.

Hazelnut Scones

Ground hazelnuts give these scones a rich texture. A touch of freshly brewed hazelnut coffee elevates them to hazelnut heaven, and the chopped hazelnuts are the icing on the cake (or the hazelnuts on the scone, as the case may be). The scones taste great still warm, topped with margarine and apple butter. I recommend brewing a whole pot of the hazelnut coffee and cooling the rest to have iced hazelnut coffee alongside your scones.

½ cup soy cream (use the hazelnut soy cream if you can find it, if not, rice or soy milk makes a fine substitution)

¾ cup freshly brewed hazelnut coffee

2 teaspoons apple cider vinegar

1 teaspoon vanilla extract

⅓ cup vegetable shortening

¼ cup sugar, plus an extra teaspoon for sprinkling the tops (optional)

2 cups all-purpose flour

2 tablespoons baking powder

¼ teaspoon salt

1 cup hazelnut meal (see Punk Points)

½ teaspoon freshly grated nutmeg

½ cup toasted and coarsely chopped hazelnuts (see Punk Points)

PUNK POINTS

Hazelnut meal is hard to find. To make your own, toast the hazelnuts on a baking sheet at 350°F for about 12 minutes. Wrap the nuts in a small kitchen towel for 2 minutes while they are still warm, then rub the nuts together so that any burnt skins come off. (This toasting and peeling method should be used for the toasted, chopped hazelnuts as well.) Transfer the nuts to a strong blender or (better yet) a food processor and pulse into a coarse powder. 1¼ cups whole hazelnuts will yield roughly 1 cup of meal.

Preheat oven to 400°F. Lightly grease a cookie sheet.

Measure out the soy cream and coffee and stir in the vinegar and vanilla extract. Set aside.

In a large bowl, cream together the shortening and sugar.

In a large mixing bowl, sift together the flour, baking powder, and salt. Add the hazelnut meal and nutmeg. Add the shortening mixture in clumps (use a teaspoon or your fingers) and mix with your fingertips or a pastry knife until the mixture resembles course crumbs. Add the coffee mixture and mix with a wooden spoon until just combined; fold in the chopped hazelnuts. The dough should be clumpy and dry; even if there is still a light dusting of flour, that is okay.

Drop by ¼ cupfuls onto the greased cookie sheet; sprinkle with a little sugar if you like. Bake 12 to 15 minutes, until slightly browned on the bottom and vegan on the top.

Glazed Orange Scones

I created this recipe specifically for my mom, who described to me the scone that she likes to get at one of those overpriced French cafés in Union Square where she works. She was really pleased with how they turned out and so was I. They are a little sweeter than the scones I usually make and they have lots of zesty orange flavor.

> ½ cup soy cream (rice or soy milk make a fine substitution)
> ¾ cup rice or soy milk
> 1 tablespoon apple cider vinegar
> 3 cups all-purpose flour
> ⅓ cup sugar
> 2 tablespoons baking powder
> ¼ teaspoon salt
> ⅓ cup vegetable oil
> 3 tablespoons finely grated orange zest
> Orange Glaze (recipe follows)

Preheat oven to 400°F. Lightly grease a cookie sheet.

In a measuring cup combine the soy cream, rice milk, and vinegar, set aside.

In a large mixing bowl, sift together the flour, sugar, baking powder, and salt. Add the rice milk mixture, oil, and orange zest; mix until just combined; the dough should be clumpy and not sticky. Even if there is still a light dusting of flour it's okay.

Divide the dough in two. Knead one portion a few times, then form into a 6-inch disk. Cut the disk into six slices, pizza-style), and place each slice on the prepared cookie sheet. Do the same with the remaining dough. Bake for 12 to 15 minutes, until slightly browned on the bottom and firm on top. Transfer to a cooling rack.

When cool (if they are still only slightly warm that is okay) transfer to parchment paper. Pour about 2 tablespoons Orange Glaze over the scones; let the tops set before eating. If you simply can't wait, prepare to have sticky fingers.

VEGAN WITH A VENGEANCE

Orange Glaze

1 cup confectioners' sugar
2 tablespoons nonhydrogenated margarine, melted
2 tablespoons fresh orange juice
1 teaspoon finely grated orange zest

Sift the confectioners' sugar into a mixing bowl; add all the other ingredients and mix until smooth.

Lemon-Poppy Seed Muffins

I made these after asking the visitors on my Web site what their favorite muffin was. Turns out it was lemon poppy seed—who knew? I had lots of happy fans after posting this.

> 1¾ cups all-purpose flour
> ¼ cup sugar
> 1 tablespoon baking powder
> ¼ teaspoon salt
> ⅓ cup canola oil
> ¾ cup rice or soy milk
> 1 (6-ounce) container soy yogurt, plain or vanilla (vanilla will make it only slightly sweeter)
> 1 teaspoon vanilla extract
> 2 tablespoons finely grated lemon zest (zest from 2 lemons)
> 1 tablespoon poppy seeds

Preheat oven to 400°F.

In a large bowl, sift together the flour, sugar, baking powder, and salt. In a separate bowl, whisk together the oil, rice milk, yogurt, and vanilla. Add the lemon zest to the wet ingredients. Fold the wet ingredients into the dry; halfway through mixing fold in the poppy seeds.

Spray a twelve-muffin tin with non-stick cooking spray. Fill each cup two-thirds full. Bake for 20 to 25 minutes, until a toothpick inserted in the center comes out clean. Serve warm.

PUNK POiNTS

To make sure you always have fresh muffins, freeze half a batch. Pour the batter into paper cupcake liners, then put them in the freezer. Once frozen, store in tightly sealed plastic containers and bake one in a muffin tin, adding an extra 8–10 minutes to the cooking time, whenever you want a muffin, no need to thaw.

VEGAN WITH A VENGEANCE

Carrot-Raisin Muffins

These are my favorite morning muffin. Since I weaned myself off of caffeine I need a little kick to wake me up. Actually, I need several really hard kicks and in some cases a bucket of ice water dumped over my head. But what I'm saying is, once I'm awake the little bit of spice to these muffins seals the deal.

½ cup raisins
1½ cups flour
2 teaspoons baking powder
½ teaspoon baking soda
½ teaspoon ground cinnamon
¼ teaspoon ground or freshly grated nutmeg
¼ cup sugar
½ teaspoon salt
1 cup rice or soy milk
¼ cup canola oil
1 teaspoon vanilla extract
2 cups grated carrot

Preheat oven to 400°F. Spray a muffin tin with nonstick cooking spray or lightly grease with oil.

Soak the raisins in a bowl of hot water and begin preparing the batter. In a large mixing bowl sift together flour, baking powder, baking soda, cinnamon, nutmeg, sugar and salt. Create a well in the center and add the milk, oil, and vanilla; mix with a wooden spoon until just combined. Fold in the grated carrots. Remove the raisins from the water and fold in.

Fill the muffin tins three-quarters full. Bake for 18 to 22 minutes, until a toothpick or knife inserted in the center of one comes out clean. Let cool on a cooling rack.

> **PUNK POINTS**
>
> Soaking the raisins in hot water gives them new life and makes them plump and juicy. Just boil some water, put the raisins in a bowl, pour the water over them, and let them sit for a good 10 minutes.

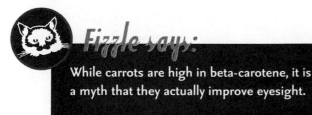

Fizzle says:

While carrots are high in beta-carotene, it is a myth that they actually improve eyesight.

VEGAN WITH VENGEANCE

Cherry-Almond Muffins

Cherries are expensive so make sure to pick only the ones that are most perfect and firm. Take your time in the store and go through the whole pile until you come to be known as "Crazy Cherry Girl/Guy" by the shopkeepers.

> 2 cups all-purpose flour
> 1/3 cup sugar
> 2 teaspoons baking powder
> 1/2 teaspoon baking soda
> 1/4 teaspoon salt
> 1/3 cup canola oil
> 3/4 cup rice or soy milk
> 1 (6-ounce) container soy yogurt, plain or vanilla (vanilla will make it only slightly sweeter)
> 2 teaspoons almond extract
> 1 cup sliced almonds
> 3/4 cup fresh bing cherries, halved and pitted

Preheat oven to 400°F. Lightly grease a twelve-muffin tin.

In a large bowl, sift together flour, sugar, baking powder, baking soda, and salt. Create a well in the center and add the oil, rice milk, yogurt, and almond extract. Mix with a wooden spoon until combined. Fold in 1/2 cup of the almonds and all of the cherries.

Fill the muffin cups three-quarters full; press the remaining slivered almonds into the tops of the muffins. Bake for 18 to 22 minutes, until a toothpick or knife inserted in the center of one comes out clean.

VEGAN WITH A VENGEANCE

Ginger-Raisin Bran Muffins

MAKES 1 DOZEN MUFFINS

These are so *tasty and healthy, too.*

½ cup raisins
1½ cups all-purpose flour
2 teaspoons baking powder
½ teaspoon baking soda
½ cup sugar
2 teaspoons ground ginger
1 teaspoon ground cinnamon
½ teaspoon salt
¾ cups bran
1¼ cups rice or soy milk
⅓ cup canola oil
1 teaspoon vanilla extract
¼ cup chopped crystallized ginger

Preheat oven to 400°F. Lightly grease a twelve-muffin tin. Soak the raisins in hot water to cover, set aside.

In a large mixing bowl sift together the flour, baking powder, baking soda, sugar, ginger, cinnamon, and salt. Mix in the bran. Create a well in the center and add the rice milk, oil, and vanilla. Mix with a wooden spoon just until combined. Drain the raisins and fold them in along with the crystallized ginger.

Fill each muffin cup most of the way full and bake for 20 to 22 minutes, until a toothpick or knife inserted in the center comes out clean.

VEGAN WITH A VENGEANCE

Sunny Blueberry-Corn Muffins

These are perfect sweet corn muffins, crispy outside and soft inside. They've got a great crumb, perfect for spreading with a pat of soy margarine. I call them sunny because of the lemon zest.

    1 cup all-purpose flour
    1 cup cornmeal
    1 tablespoon baking powder
    ½ teaspoon salt
    ⅓ cup sugar
    ½ cup corn or vegetable oil
    ¾ cup soy milk
    2 tablespoons soy yogurt
    1 teaspoon vanilla extract
    Finely grated zest of 1 lemon
     1¼ cups blueberries

Preheat oven to 400°F. Lightly grease a twelve-muffin tin.

In a large bowl, sift together the flour, cornmeal, baking powder, salt, and sugar. In a separate bowl, whisk together the oil, soy milk, soy yogurt, vanilla, and lemon zest. With a wooden spoon, fold the wet ingredients into the dry. Fold in the blueberries, being careful not to overmix.

Fill each muffin cup three-quarters full. Bake for 20 to 25 minutes, until a toothpick or knife inserted in the center of one comes out clean. Serve warm.

PUNK POINTS

To keep the blueberries from sinking to the bottom of the muffin, toss them around in a bowl of flour to coat. That will give them some "grip" in the batter.

MUFFINS AND SCONES

VEGAN WITH A VENGEANCE

Mocha Chip Muffins

Here I go and break my own rule and make a muffin that is more like dessert. So sue me. I use powdered instant coffee because I think its coffee flavor remains truer than that of fresh-brewed coffee. If you don't have any instant coffee, just use an extra tablespoon of cocoa powder and have a chocolate-chocolate chip muffin.

    1½ cups all-purpose flour
    ¾ cup sugar
    ¼ cup cocoa powder
    2½ teaspoons baking powder
    ½ teaspoon salt
    2 teaspoons instant coffee powder
    1 cup soy milk
    ½ cup canola oil
    3 tablespoons soy yogurt
    1 teaspoon vanilla extract
    ½ cup chocolate chips

Preheat oven to 375°F. Lightly grease a twelve-muffin tin.

In a large bowl, sift together flour, sugar, cocoa powder, baking powder, and salt. Mix in the instant coffee powder.

In a separate bowl, whisk together the soy milk, oil, yogurt, and vanilla.

Pour the wet ingredients into the dry and mix until the dry ingredients are moistened. Fold in the chocolate chips. Fill the muffin cups three-quarters full. Bake 18 to 20 minutes, or until a toothpick or knife inserted into the center of one comes out clean.

VEGAN WITH A VENGEANCE

The Best Pumpkin Muffins

Everyone loves these muffins. (You think I throw around phrases like "The Best" for nothing?) I created them when I was baking for a café and they sold like nobody's business. They truly are perfect in every way.

1¾ cups all-purpose flour
1¼ cups sugar
1 tablespoon baking powder
¼ teaspoon salt
1 teaspoon ground cinnamon
½ teaspoon ground or freshly grated nutmeg
½ teaspoon ground ginger
¼ teaspoon ground allspice
⅛ teaspoon ground cloves
1 cup pureed pumpkin (Fresh or from a can; do not use pumpkin pie mix)
½ cup soy milk
½ cup vegetable oil
2 tablespoons molasses

Preheat oven to 400°F. Lightly grease a twelve-muffin tin.

Sift together flour, sugar, baking powder, salt, and spices. In a separate bowl, whisk together pumpkin, soy milk, oil, and molasses. Pour the wet ingredients into the dry and mix.

Fill the muffin cups two-thirds full. Bake for 18 to 20 minutes, until a toothpick or knife inserted in the center comes out clean.

VARIATION

Fold in a cup of either chopped fresh cranberries or chopped walnuts, or a mixture of the two.

Apple Pie–Crumb Cake Muffins

The grated and chopped apples create an apple pie filling in the center of the muffin. It's a nice surprise to an already sweet and spicy treat.

FOR MUFFINS:

1½ cups flour

¼ cup plus 2 tablespoons sugar

1 teaspoon baking powder

1 teaspoon baking soda

1 teaspoon ground cinnamon

½ teaspoon ground allspice

⅛ teaspoon ground cloves

¼ teaspoon salt

¾ cup apple cider

⅓ cup canola oil

1 teaspoon vanilla extract

½ cup grated apple

½ cup chopped apple (¼-inch pieces)

FOR TOPPING:

¼ cup all-purpose flour

¼ cup brown sugar

½ teaspoon ground cinnamon

¼ teaspoon ground allspice

Pinch of salt

3 tablespoons canola oil

Prepare the topping by mixing all the dry topping ingredients together in a small bowl. Drizzle the oil in while mixing with your fingertips until crumbs form. Set aside.

Preheat oven to 375°F, lightly grease a twelve-muffin tin.

In a large mixing bowl, sift together the flour, sugar, baking powder, baking soda, spices, and salt. Create a well in the center and add the apple cider, oil, and vanilla. Mix, then fold in the grated and chopped apple.

Fill each muffin cup two-thirds full. Sprinkle the crumb topping over each muffin. Bake for 22 minutes.

VEGAN WITH A VENGEANCE

Sometimes I double these recipes and make a big batch to either freeze or eat throughout the week. I love making soup for several reasons, like it's delicious and fast, but the biggest impetus is that everything goes in one pot and there aren't a gazillion dishes to clean up (or let sit in the sink for a week) afterward. All of these soup recipes are hearty enough to be meals, with some rice or good crusty bread.

SOUPS

Carrot Bisque

I've never been crazy about carrot soups, they always seemed a little too skimpy and health-foody for me. But this slightly sweet, incredibly creamy and hearty carrot soup changed all that. It's easy to make, to boot.

> 3 pounds carrots, peeled and diced into a little smaller than ½-inch pieces
> 1 large onion, chopped
> 2 tablespoons peanut oil (vegetable oil will do)
> 2 cloves garlic, minced
> 1 tablespoon curry powder
> ½ teaspoon salt
> A few dashes fresh black pepper
> 3 cups vegetable broth, or 1 bouillon cube dissolved in 3 cups water
> 1 (13-ounce) can coconut milk
> 1 tablespoon maple syrup

In a stockpot over low-medium heat, cook the carrots and onions in the peanut oil for 7 to 10 minutes; cover and stir occasionally. You want the onions to brown but not to burn, although if they burn a little bit it's not the end of the world. Add the garlic, curry, salt, and pepper; sauté for 1 more minute. Add the 3 cups of broth, cover, and bring to a boil. Lower the heat and simmer for 10 to 12 minutes, or until the carrots are tender.

Add the coconut milk and bring to a low boil. Turn the heat off. Use a handheld blender to puree half of the soup; if you don't have one, then puree half the soup in a blender and add it back to the soup pot (see Punk Point). Add the maple syrup and stir. Serve hot.

PUNK POINTS

If you are using a blender to puree the soup, let the soup cool a bit so that the steam doesn't cause the blender lid to pop off and hot soup to splatter everywhere. Once the soup has cooled, give it a few pulses in the blender, lift the lid to let steam escape, and repeat.

VEGAN WITH A VENGEANCE

Corn Chowder

Fresh, sweet corn, especially in the summer when it's in season, has such a pure taste I sometimes just like to just eat it raw. Potatoes give this soup a creamy, hearty body and the jalapeños give it just a little kick.

- 1 tablespoon olive oil
- 1 medium-size onion, cut into ¼-inch dice
- 1 large red bell pepper, finely chopped (about 1½ cups)
- 1 cup carrots, peeled and cut into ½-inch dice
- 2 jalapeño peppers, seeded and thinly sliced (use just one if you like less heat)
- 1 teaspoon dried rosemary
- 1 teaspoon dried thyme
- A few dashes fresh black pepper
- 1 teaspoon salt
- 3 cups vegetable broth or water
- 3 cups fresh corn kernels (from about 5 ears of corn)
- 2 medium-size russet potatoes, peeled and sliced into ½-inch chunks
- 1 bay leaf
- Pinch cayenne
- Juice of 1 lime
- ¼ cup plain soy milk
- 1 tablespoon maple syrup

In stockpot sauté the onions, bell peppers, carrots, and jalapeños in the olive oil over medium heat until the onions are translucent, about 7 minutes. Add rosemary, thyme, black pepper, and salt; sauté 1 minute more. Add the broth, corn, potatoes, bay leaf, and cayenne. Cover and bring to a boil, then lower the heat and simmer for 20 minutes, or until the potatoes are tender. Uncover and simmer 10 minutes more to let the liquid reduce a bit.

Remove the bay leaf and puree half the chowder either using a handheld blender or by transferring half the chowder to a blender, pureeing till smooth (see Punk Point on page 56), and adding back to soup. Add the lime juice to taste, and the soy milk and maple syrup, and simmer 5 more minutes. Let sit for at least 10 minutes and serve. Tastes even better the next day.

Beet, Barley, and Black Soybean Soup with Pumpernickel Croutons

We created a soup like this for Food Not Bombs, in San Francisco, and I will always remember how happy it made everyone (except for my roommate who was pissed at me for dumping a whole bottle of her tamari into the soup. She was also pissed at me for not paying rent but that's another matter entirely). Eating this soup makes me think I am in Mother Russia in the late nineteenth century; I've come home after strolling the promenade in Saint Petersburg and I'm getting ready to complete the next chapter of my tragic novel, but first—soup.

2 tablespoons olive oil
1 large onion, finely chopped (about 2 cups)
3 cloves garlic
2 teaspoons dried tarragon
A few dashes fresh black pepper
8 cups water
4 medium-size beets, peeled, cut in half, sliced ¼-inch thick (about 4 cups)
¾ cup pearl barley
¼ cup tamari
1 (15-ounce) can black soybeans, rinsed and drained (about 2 cups)
2 tablespoons balsamic vinegar
½ cup chopped fresh dill
Pumpernickel Croutons (recipe follows)

In a stockpot over medium heat, sauté the onion in the olive oil for 5 minutes. Add the garlic, tarragon, and pepper; sauté until fragrant (about a minute). Add 8 cups of water, the beets, barley, and tamari, cover, and bring to a boil. Lower the heat and simmer for 30 minutes. Add the beans and simmer for another 10 to 15 minutes, stirring frequently to prevent the barley from sticking together, or until the barley is tender. Add the balsamic vinegar and fresh dill. Serve with Pumpernickel Croutons, and garnish with more fresh dill.

Pumpernickel Croutons

    2 tablespoons extra-virgin olive oil
    ½ teaspoon dried tarragon
    ¼ teaspoon salt
    4 slices firm pumpernickel bread, cut into ¼-inch dice

Preheat oven to 400°F.

In a wide, shallow bowl, stir together the olive oil, tarragon, and salt. Add the diced bread and toss gently to coat. Spread the bread in a single layer on a cookie sheet, toast for 8 to 10 minutes, stirring once. Remove from oven and let cool.

VEGAN WITH A VENGEANCE

Chipotle, Corn, and Black Bean Stew

This is one of the recipes that you can really mess around with; add zucchini or cauliflower or whatever vegetables you have around. You can also try different beans; pintos or garbanzos are nice choices. I also like to add tempeh or frozen and thawed tofu sometimes, at the same time you add the potatoes. Let the soup sit for at least 10 minutes before serving—the longer you can wait, the better. If you want to make the soup less spicy, remove the seeds from the chipotles before using.

2 tablespoons olive oil
1 large onion, quartered and thinly sliced
3 cloves garlic
2 teaspoons ground cumin
½ teaspoons salt
A few dashes fresh black pepper
2 chipotle peppers (canned), drained and chopped
1 (28-ounce) can crushed tomatoes
3 cups water
4 russet potatoes, cut into ¾-inch dice
2 carrots, peeled, cut into ¾-inch dice
1 cup corn (if using fresh, it's 2 ears)
1 (16-ounce) can black beans, drained and rinsed
1 cup fresh cilantro, lightly packed, torn into pieces (stems and all)
Finely grated zest of 1 lime
Juice of 1 lime

Fizzle says:

Chipotle peppers are smoked jalapeños.

In a stockpot, sauté the onions in the oil over moderate heat for 5 minutes. Add the garlic, cumin, salt, and black pepper. Sauté 1 minute more. Add the chipotles, tomatoes and water, stir. Add the potatoes and carrots, cover, bring to a low boil, and simmer for 20 minutes

VEGAN WITH A VENGEANCE

Uncover, add the corn and beans. Thin with more water if needed. Cook uncovered for 5 more minutes. Add the cilantro, lime zest, and lime juice. Let sit for at least 10 minutes. Serve. (If you can wait an hour to eat it, it tastes so good when it's had a chance to sit around and is gently reheated.)

PUNK POINTS

Be very careful when working with hot peppers, the white lining in the pepper contains a chemical called capsaicin, which gives the pepper its heat. Don't ever touch the inside of the pepper with your bare hands or they will burn for hours and sometimes even the next day (if you touch your eyes, you'll feel like you were just maced by the police at a Critical Mass demo). Either work very carefully with a small paring knife or employ a pair of disposable gloves while cutting and chopping.

VEGAN WITH A VENGEANCE

Roasted Butternut Squash Soup

Roasting the squash intensifies its sweetness but be careful not to eat it all before you have a chance to make the soup. The ingredients here are simple yet the results are scrumptious.

> 5 pounds butternut squash (about 3), peeled, bulbous part cut from the stem part, then each part sliced in half, seeds removed
> 4 tablespoons olive oil
> 1 medium-size yellow onion, diced
> 1 serrano chile, chopped (any chile will do, or you can omit if you don't want it spicy at all)
> 1 tablespoon grated fresh ginger
> 3 cloves garlic, minced
> 1 teaspoon salt (or more to taste)
> 4 cups vegetable stock, or 2 cubes vegetable bouillon dissolved in 4 cups water
> 1 tablespoon maple syrup
> Juice of 1 or 2 limes, to taste

Preheat oven to 425°F.

Lightly coat the squash halves with 2 tablespoons of the olive oil and place cut side down on a nonstick or parchment-lined rimmed baking sheet (if you don't have a rimmed baking sheet then use baking pans, to prevent the oil from dripping and starting a grease fire). Bake for 40 to 45 minutes, or until the squash is tender and easily pierced with a fork.

When the squash is about 15 minutes from being done, in a stockpot over medium heat sauté the onions in the remaining 2 tablespoons of olive oil for 5 minutes. Add the chiles; sauté 5 minutes more. Lastly, add the ginger, garlic, and salt; sauté 2 minutes more.

When squash is ready, puree in a blender or food processor along with the vegetable broth and sautéed onion, until smooth. Return the mixture to the pot and heat through, add the maple syrup and lime juice, and serve.

VEGAN WITH A VENGEANCE

My top-secret technique for prepping a butternut squash: First, peel the whole thing with a serrated peeler, if you have one-it does a good job of slicing off the hard skin. Cut the squash in half widthwise, separating the bulbous part from the long part. Place the bulbous part cut-side down and slice it in half, then use a tablespoon to remove the seeds and the stringy bits. You should then be able to cut the squash into smaller pieces. Next, slice the long part of the squash in half and then cut into whatever size pieces you need. All too often I watch people struggle with this gourd, trying to cut it in half in one fell swoop and then peel it. I hope this has cleared things up for those of you who don't like cooking butternut squash because it's too difficult (I'm talkin' to you, Mom).

VEGAN WITH A
VENGEANCE

Food Not Bombs is a loosely knit network of activists that get together on a regular basis to cook food and feed people. Groups exist all across the world. Much more than Meals on Wheels, it's a social movement that has been growing since 1980.

In the late '80s and early '90s, a group of us would get together on Sundays and go from store to store gathering food donations. In many cases, it was food that would otherwise have been discarded—blemished vegetables from the greengrocers or day-old bagels from the bagel shops. We'd haul everything over to Lucky 13—a squat on 13th Street that had been around forever and was cool enough to host punk shows and let strangers use their kitchen—in a shopping cart "donated" by the local Key Food. There we would concoct hearty vats of vegetarian soup over a few hot plates, using water we tapped from the fire hydrant down the block (I'm not kidding).

When the soups were done, everything would be piled back into the shopping cart and rolled a few blocks to Tompkins Square Park. The crowd we fed was diverse: yippies, homeless, junkies, psychopaths, artists, squatters, punks, and some combinations of the above. This was during the time of the Tompkins Square Park riots; activists were fighting to keep a curfew off the park and a shantytown called Tent City was set up on the lawn as a home for dozens of people. It was a rather dystopian scene. Cops milled about, and it was anyone's guess as to whether they would decide to arrest us on a given evening. Despite these drawbacks, conversation was always lively and the food was always appreciated.

One of the greatest things about Food Not Bombs was that you could go to virtually any city and get involved. The experience was always different from place to place. In San Francisco I was shocked to see how organized they were. They had a van! They had folding tables and a banner! In Berkeley they cooked in a college dorm and served scones that were donated by a bakery. In Minneapolis they seemed to serve exclusively punks. In Baltimore they served in the inner cities and I bore witness to the sort of urban decay usually saved for postapocalyptic movies.

If I had to name a time and place, I would say that cooking for FNB was where I gained my knife skills as I chopped scores and scores of vegetables. It also influenced my cooking for years to come. For a long time it was nearly impossible for me to cook normal portions of food.

It is easy to start your own Food Not Bombs, or join an existing one, and feed people in your community. Check their Web site for more information: www.foodnot-bombs.com.

If distributed equally, the world produces enough food to feed everyone. There is an abundance of food. In fact, in this country, every day, in every city, far more edible food is discarded than is needed to feed those who do not have enough to eat.

Consider this. Before food reaches your table, it is produced and handled by farmers, coops, manufacturers, distributors, wholesalers, and retailers. At every step, some perfectly edible food is discarded for a variety of business reasons. In the average city, approximately 10% of all solid waste is food. Nationally, this is an incredible total of 46 billion pounds per year, just under 200 pounds per person per year . . .

—From the Food Not Bombs Web site

Potato-Asparagus Soup

I didn't spice this up too much because asparagus is my favorite vegetable and I like its flavor to shine through. I like to add some fresh dill to each serving but it's completely optional. If you like a chunkier soup, then just puree half of the soup, or use a handheld blender and puree to your liking.

3 pounds russet potatoes, peeled, cut into 1-inch chunks
1 pound asparagus, rough ends discarded, tips cut into 2-inch pieces, lower part
    cut into ½-inch pieces
2 tablespoons olive oil
1 large onion, cut into ½-inch dice
3 cloves garlic, minced
1 teaspoon salt
A few dashes fresh black pepper
4 cups vegetable broth, or 2 bouillon cubes dissolved in 4 cups water
2 bay leaves
Juice of 1 lemon
¼ cup chopped fresh dill

Place potatoes in a stockpot and cover with cold water. Cover the pot and bring to a boil, then lower the heat and simmer for 20 minutes or until tender. Add the asparagus, boil for 3 minutes, drain, and set aside.

Rinse out the pot, then in the same pot sauté the onion in the olive oil for 5 to 7 minutes; add the garlic, salt and black pepper,; and sauté 2 more minutes. Add the broth and bay leaves, boil for 10 minutes, discard the bay leaves. Add the potatoes and asparagus, heat through, then puree three-quarters of the soup in a blender or food processor (see Punk Points on page 56). Reheat if necessary. Add a squeeze of lemon and serve garnished with fresh dill.

VEGAN WITH A VENGEANCE

White Bean and Roasted Garlic Soup

Serve this with garlic croutons or a nice peasant bread. When you eat this soup you will be transported to a rustic villa in Italy where the air is clean and fresh, the locals are provincial but friendly, and you have the solitude you need to finish your sonnets. If you have never roasted garlic before, you don't know what you are missing; it adds a great depth of flavor. I like to think of it as a "restaurant taste" for lack of a better phrase.

2 tablespoons olive oil
1 medium-size onion, chopped (about
   1½ cups)
1 teaspoon salt
A few dashes fresh black pepper
½ teaspoon fennel seeds, crushed
4 cups vegetable broth, or 2 bouillon
   cubes dissolved in 4 cups water
3 cups cooked great northern (white)
   beans, drained (or canned beans,
   drained and rinsed)
3 fresh sage leaves, chopped
1 bay leaf
Juice of ½ lemon, or to taste
2 heads garlic, roasted (see Punk Points)

PUNK POINTS

TO ROAST GARLIC: Preheat oven to 350°F. Peel off as much of the papery skin as you can and put the garlic in the oven for about 30 minutes. Remove from oven and, when cool, squeeze the garlic out or peel the skin away from each clove.

In a stockpot over medium-high heat sauté the onions in the olive oil for 5 to 7 minutes.

Add the salt, black pepper, and fennel seeds; sauté for 1 minute. Add the broth, beans, sage, and bay leaf, bring to a boil, then lower the heat and simmer uncovered for 5 minutes. Remove the bay leaf. Add the roasted garlic and puree in batches in a blender or preferably a food processor (see Punk Points on page 56). Return to the pot and add lemon juice. Serve garnished with fresh fennel leaves if you have some, and/or some peeled carrot and/or parsley.

VEGAN WITH VENGEANCE

Chili sin Carne al Mole

This is Terry Hope Romero's recipe and I am a better woman for having tried it. The chocolate gives the chili a traditional mole flavor that is otherworldly. Terry tells us, "I like thick, chunky bean and vegetable-filled vegetarian chili as much as the next guy, but I've always had a longing for a meatless version of the more traditional Mexican-style chili con carne—a dark red broth, large chunks of meat, accompanied only by a few bits of onions, chiles, and spices. Seitan is ideal for this recipe, but being a meatless version it would seem rather stark without the addition of good old pinto beans. The consistency is more like a very chunky, thick soup than your usual stewlike chili. Like most soups and stews, this chili tastes even better reheated the next day."

⅓ cup olive oil
1 large onion, chopped
1 small jalapeño, minced
1 small red bell pepper, chopped
3 cloves garlic, smashed
1 pound seitan, coarsley chopped into ¼-inch cubes
2 tablespoons chile powder
1 teaspoon ground cinnamon
½ teaspoon ground cumin
1 (28-ounce) can whole, peeled tomatoes in sauce
3 tablespoons cocoa powder
3 tablespoons blackstrap molasses
2 (14-ounce) cans pinto beans, drained and well rinsed
2½ cups vegetable broth

Preheat a Dutch oven (cast iron if you have it) or large pot (at least 6-quart) over medium-high heat; pour in and heat the olive oil. Add the onions and peppers and sauté for 2 minutes; then add the garlic and seitan. Cook for 8 minutes, until onions are soft. Add the chile powder, cinnamon, and cumin, stirring constantly for another minute. Add the tomatoes, cocoa powder, and molasses. Stir and break up the tomatoes with back of a spoon, then add the beans and vegetable broth. Cover and bring to a gentle boil, then lower the heat and simmer for about 30 minutes. Allow to sit at least 20 minutes before serving.

VEGAN WITH A VENGEANCE

Curried Split Pea Soup

This is a nice and simple yet flavorful soup. Serve it as an entrée with some jasmine rice or as the perfect starter to an Indian meal. You will be surprised and relieved at how easy it is to prepare.

> 1 tablespoon olive oil
> 1 medium-size white onion, cut into ¼-inch dice
> 3 cloves garlic, minced
> 2 tablespoons fresh ginger, minced
> 2 teaspoons curry powder
> 1 teaspoon ground cumin
> ¼ teaspoon ground coriander
> ¼ teaspoon ground cardamom
> A generous pinch cinnamon
> 2 teaspoons salt
> 8 cups water
> 1 pound dried split peas
> 1 carrot
> Fresh cilantro for garnish (optional)

In a stockpot, sauté the onions in the olive oil over medium heat for about 5 minutes. Add the garlic, ginger, spices, and salt. Sauté for 2 more minutes.

Add the water and stir well. Add the split peas. Cover and bring to a boil.

Bring heat back down to medium; simmer for about an hour, until the peas are tender. Grate in the carrot and serve. You can garnish with fresh cilantro if you have it on hand.

VEGAN WITH VENGEANCE

Matzoh Ball Soup

I could write a novel on everything it took for me to perfect this recipe, but instead I will just give you the beautiful results. These are perfect light, fluffy, and flavorful matzoh dumplings. Use homemade vegetable stock to add tons of love and flavor. I suggest making the Vegetable Broth (page 72) the night before. You can even make the matzoh mixture the night before, and the big day will be a breeze.

You can halve the recipe or even third it if you aren't serving the whole mespuchah. If you don't have a huge stockpot (I use a 16-quart) then halve the recipe or boil the matzoh balls in two sessions. I make my own matzoh meal by grinding the matzoh in a food processor (it takes about six sheets to get the 1½ cups called for in this recipe) but store-bought will work just as well.

> 1½ cups matzoh meal
> ¾ teaspoon salt, plus extra for the boiling water
> ¾ teaspoon ground black pepper
> 1 (12-ounce) package firm silken tofu (like Mori-nu)
> 8½ cups or so Rich Vegetable Broth (recipe follows)
> ¼ cup plus 2 tablespoons extra-virgin olive oil
> 1 carrot, peeled
> A handful fresh dill, coarsely chopped
> Fresh parsley for garnish

In a mixing bowl, combine the matzoh meal with the salt and pepper; set aside.

Crumble the tofu into a blender or food processor, add ½ cup of the vegetable broth, and puree until smooth. Add the oil and blend again.

Mix the tofu mixture with the matzoh meal, making sure that everything is moist. Grate half the carrot into the mixture and mix until it's well distributed. Cover the bowl with plastic wrap and refrigerate for at least an hour and up to overnight. You can't skip this step; it's important in making sure that the matzoh balls will not fall apart when boiled.

When you are ready to form the balls, fill a large stockpot with enough water to fit all the matzoh balls with minimal touching. Salt the water generously, cover, and bring to a boil.

Set out a cutting board upon which to line up the formed matzoh balls, and cover it with parchment paper if you have any, to prevent sticking. Also have handy a wet rag to wipe your hands on between forming each matzoh ball.

Remove the matzoh mixture from the fridge. Form into tightly packed, walnut-size balls and place on the prepared cutting board. When all the balls are prepared, drop carefully into the boiling water, one or two at a time, with a spatula or slotted spoon. Take your time and be careful not to plop one on top of another; they need to remain separate. When all the balls are in the water, cover the pot and DO NOT LIFT LID FOR FORTY MINUTES! Sorry for the caps, just had to stress it. When the 40 minutes are up, you can remove the lid. The matzoh balls will have floated to the top and will drop back down when lid is lifted. This is fun to watch.

Now they are ready to serve; however, to make them even lighter, you can turn off the heat, cover the pot again, and let them sit in the water for another hour or so. This way they absorb more water and expand a bit more.

Prepare the remaining 8 cups of broth by placing it in a separate pot. Grate the other half of the carrot into the broth, along with a healthy handful of fresh dill. Bring to a low boil, and when it's just heated you're ready to prepare the bowls.

With a slotted spoon, carefully remove the matzoh balls from their pot and place two or three in each bowl. Ladle the broth over the matzoh balls, so that they're covered only about halfway. You can garnish with some more fresh dill, or parsley. Serve to whomever you love.

If you are not serving the soup right away, you can refrigerate the matzoh balls overnight, and boil them when ready to prepare the soup. Some people even freeze leftovers, but I never have as there've never been leftovers.

VEGAN WITH
VENGEANCE

Rich Vegetable Broth

MAKES ABOUT 8 CUPS

I make this broth to use with my matzoh ball soup. You can use other veggies, such as celery, squash, potatoes, or mushrooms; just make sure there is enough water to cover everything. Keep the skins on the onions for added color and flavor. You can also try other herbs, like thyme, rosemary, bay leaves, and peppercorns, for a stronger broth.

> 1 tablespoon olive oil
> 1 large onion, skin included, coarsely chopped
> 2 large carrots, peeled and coarsely chopped
> 2 parsnips, peeled and coarsely chopped
> 3 cloves garlic, smashed
> 2 leeks, well rinsed and coarsely chopped
> 1 cup loosely packed fresh parsley
> 1 cup loosely packed fresh dill
> 9 cups water
> 1 teaspoon salt

In a large stockpot, heat the oil. Sauté the onions for about 5 minutes on medium heat. Add all other ingredients and bring to a boil. Reduce the heat and let simmer for 1½ hours, uncovered.

Let the broth cool till it's an okay temperature to handle. Strain into a large bowl through cheesecloth or a very fine-mesh strainer. Press the vegetables with a gentle but firm pressure to get all the moisture out.

This will keep in the fridge in a tightly sealed container for up to 3 days, or freeze for up to 3 months.

These can be considered appetizers, snacks, or in some cases hors d'oeuvres. They are all great things to bring to a potluck or to cook when you have friends over for board game night (everyone has a board game night, right? Or am I just getting old?).

LITTLE MEALS, SAMMICHES, AND FINGER FOODS

Fresh Corn Fritters

These are really fast and yummy. The jalapeño and red pepper make the pancakes colorful and add just a little spice. If you don't have a red bell pepper laying around, just leave it out. Serve with salsa or as a breakfast side dish in place of potatoes. A cast-iron skillet works best for even frying.

6 ounces extra-firm silken tofu (½ package of the vacuum-packed kind)
1 tablespoon pure maple syrup
2 tablespoons soy milk
¼ cup all-purpose flour
3 ears corn, kernels cut from the cob (see Punk Points) (about 1½ cups)
¼ teaspoon salt
Several dashes fresh black pepper
1 jalapeño, very finely chopped
¼ red bell pepper, very finely chopped
Corn oil for frying (canola or any light vegetable oil will do)

In a blender or food processor whiz the tofu, maple syrup, and soy milk, scraping down the sides with a rubber spatula often, until everything is smooth. Add half the corn (¾ cup) and pulse about 20 times (scraping down the sides after 10 times), so that the mixture is chunky. Transfer to a bowl, add the rest of the ingredients (except for the oil), and combine well.

Heat a thin layer of oil in a heavy skillet over medium-high. Drop the batter by table-spoonfuls into the skillet. Flatten a little with the back of the spoon (wet the spoon first to avoid sticking). Cook 2½ to 3 minutes on each side, until lightly browned. I do this in two batches. When done, rest on a brown paper bag or paper towels to drain the oil.

PUNK POINTS

To cut the corn from the cob, place the shucked corn pointy side up on a kitchen or paper towel. Take a chef's knife and cut downward, as close as you can to the cob. The towel will keep the corn kernels from bouncing everywhere and also makes a handy vehicle for transporting them to the mixing bowl.

74 | LITTLE MEALS, SAMMICHES, AND FINGER FOODS

VEGAN WITH A VENGEANCE

My Childhood in Yellow Cabs and Knishes

When I was a child, my father was a NYC cabbie. Like so many children of divorced parents I only saw him on the weekends but the thing was he worked on the weekends, so I got to drive around in the taxi with him. He would stack two phone books on the front seat for me to sit on, so that I could look out the window. This was the NYC I loved as a child: bright, dangerous, and loud. Looking out the window was like watching a movie, so many different kinds of people. My dad cursed at most of the passengers when they'd give a lousy tip, which made the rides even more colorful for me. At the time the Lower East Side was still teeming with Jewish culture and my dad knew all the best places for a quick nosh. Among them was Yonah Shimmel knishes on Houston Street.

Today the neighborhood is pretty much a hipster shopping mall but miraculously Yonah Shimmel is still there, and its delicious knishes still line the window. I think of my dad whenever I pass and I long for that NYC I knew as a child. I can only imagine the NYC my parents remember. I like to stop in once in a while and get nostalgic for a time that I knew and those old days that I didn't know.

Knish Madness:
Three Kinds of Knishes— Sweet Potato, Potato, and Spinach-Potato

MAKES 15 GOOD-SIZE KNISHES

I brought these to Rosh Hashanah dinner at my aunt's one year and everyone loved them until she started telling people that they were vegan, then all of a sudden no one would touch them. Actually, most knish recipes are vegan. I like to make all three fillings because it's easy to do and the colors look really cool together. The real work here is the dough, which you have to knead for a long time to get it smooth and stretchy enough; after that you are halfway to knish madness. There are a lot of steps but actually not so much active prep/cooking time, so don't be intimidated.

FOR THE DOUGH:
- 1 medium-size russet potato
- 2 tablespoons olive oil, plus extra for brushing
- ¾ cup cold water
- 1 teaspoon salt
- 1 teaspoon baking powder
- 3 cups all-purpose flour

FOR THE FILLINGS:
- 1 large yellow onion, finely chopped (about 2 cups)
- 4 tablespoons olive oil
- 6 medium-size russet potatoes
- 1 teaspoon salt
- ¼ teaspoon ground black pepper
- 1 (10-ounce) package frozen spinach, thawed and drained (drain while potatoes bake)
- 4 medium-size sweet potatoes (about 2 pounds)
- ¼ teaspoon ground or freshly grated nutmeg
- ¼ teaspoon ground cinnamon
- ¼ teaspoon ground allspice

Preheat oven to 350°F. Prick the seven regular potatoes with a fork and wrap in foil and place in the oven. The four sweet potatoes can just go in as is. Take out the sweet potatoes after 40 minutes; the regular potatoes will need to bake another 30 minutes, so they will take about 70 minutes total, depending on their size. Remove from the oven and let cool.

76 | LITTLE MEALS, SAMMICHES, AND FINGER FOODS

To make the dough:

In a large bowl, place one peeled baked potato for the dough, let the others continue to cool. Add the oil and water to the potato and mash until well combined. Add the salt and baking powder, and then add the flour in batches, kneading with each addition. Knead until you have a smooth dough. This can take up to 15 minutes, so have someone nearby to help knead in case your little hands get tired. Let the dough rest while you prepare the fillings.

For potato knishes:

Sauté the onions in 2 tablespoons of the olive oil over medium heat for 15 minutes, until browned and slightly caramelized.

Mash the six peeled, baked russet potatoes in a large bowl. Add the cooked onions, the remaining 2 tablespoons of olive oil, and salt and pepper to taste. Mash together well.

For spinach knishes:

Add the thawed, drained spinach to half of the potato mixture and mix until well combined.

For sweet potato knishes:

Mash the baked sweet potatoes. Add ¼ teaspoon each ginger, nutmeg, cinnamon and salt, and mix well.

To assemble and bake the knishes:

Cut the dough into three equal portions. Roll one portion out as thinly as possible, into a 14 × 6-inch rectangle. It won't be a perfect rectangle, more of an oval, and that is fine. Sprinkle with flour as you roll to keep the dough unsticky.

Place 2½ cups of a single filling down the center of the rolled-out portion of dough. Spread out so that the filling is roughly 12 × 2 inches. Fold the dough over the filling the long way to create a roll. Trim the ends of the roll up to where the filling begins. Place folded side down on lightly greased baking sheet.

Repeat with the other two portions of dough and the other two fillings. (You may have extra filling, depending on how big your potatoes were. Don't overstuff the knishes, just bite the bullet and eat the filling on its own.)

With a knife, score each roll into fifths. That will give them a nice shape and make them easier to cut when they are done. Brush each lightly with olive oil. Bake at 350°F for 40 minutes.

Remove from oven; let cool just enough so that you can slice them. Serve warm, with plenty of mustard for the potato and spinach ones.

Olive, Tomato, and Millet-Stuffed Zucchini

Zucchini boats are perfect vehicles for transporting the tangy olive-tomato-millet combination into your mouth.

1 medium-size onion, finely chopped
1 tablespoon olive oil
2 cloves garlic, minced
½ cup millet, rinsed
A few dashes fresh black pepper
½ teaspoon dried rosemary
½ teaspoon dried thyme
½ teaspoon dried marjoram
½ teaspoon dried basil
1 teaspoon paprika
½ teaspoon salt
1 (22-ounce) can whole tomatoes
2 cups vegetable broth or water
4 medium-size zucchini, ends trimmed
½ cup chopped, pitted kalamata olives
¼ cup capers
Chopped fresh parsley for garnish

Sauté the onions in the olive oil over moderate heat for 5 to 7 minutes, until the onions are translucent. Add the garlic and sauté until fragrant, about a minute.

Add the millet, herbs, spices, and salt; sauté for about 3 minutes. Add the tomatoes, crushing them with your hands as you add them. Add the remaining tomato juice and vegetable broth. Cover the pot and bring to a boil, then lower the heat and simmer for 20 minutes.

Meanwhile, prepare the zucchini: Slice in half lengthwise. Place in a large saucepan cut side down, fill the pan with enough water to cover the zucchini halfway. Cover the pan, bring to a boil, then cook for 5 minutes. Remove the zucchini from the water and place on a plate to cool. Once cool enough to handle, use a tablespoon to remove their pulp, leaving only about ¼ inch of pulp in the zucchini. Chop the removed pulp and reserve.

VEGAN WITH A VENGEANCE

Preheat oven to 350°F.

Add the zucchini pulp, olives, and capers to the millet mixture. Simmer for about 5 more minutes, until the millet is tender.

Stuff each zucchini half with some of the mixture. Place in a baking dish and bake for about 20 minutes. Let cool about 5 minutes before serving.

VEGAN WITH VENGEANCE

Potato-Edamame Samosas with Coconut-Mint Chutney

Samosas are crispy pockets of dough, stuffed with a rich and flavorful filling. I can't imagine starting any Indian meal without them. Most New Yorkers are familiar with the strip of Indian restaurants on 6th Street that try to lure you in with Christmas lights and promises of the best samosas, but all too often these samosas are an oily mess that have been sitting under a heat lamp for far too long. The samosas I make are baked not fried, and I opt to use edamame instead of peas for a more toothsome bite, although you can stick with green peas if you're all about tradition. Serve with Coconut-Mint Chutney (recipe follows).

FOR THE DOUGH:

¾ cup rice or soy milk

¼ cup vegetable oil

1 tablespoon apple cider vinegar (any mild vinegar will do)

About 3 cups all-purpose flour

¼ teaspoon ground turmeric

¼ teaspoon baking powder

1 teaspoon salt

FOR THE FILLING:

3 medium-size russet potatoes, peeled and cut into 1-inch chunks

2 tablespoons vegetable oil plus extra for brushing

1 teaspoon cumin seeds

2 teaspoons mustard seeds

1 medium-size yellow onion, very finely chopped

1 cup finely diced carrots,

2 cloves garlic, minced

1 tablespoon fresh ginger, minced

1 teaspoon ground coriander

½ teaspoon ground turmeric

Pinch of cayenne pepper

1 teaspoon salt

Juice of 1 lemon

¾ cup shelled frozen edamame or green peas

VEGAN WITH A VENGEANCE

In a saucepan, boil the potatoes until tender, 20 to 25 minutes. When they are ready, drain and set aside.

Preheat oven to 400°F. Meanwhile, prepare the dough.

To make the dough:

Pour the wet dough ingredients into a mixing bowl. Add 2 cups of the flour, and the turmeric, baking powder, and salt. Begin kneading the mixture, adding the rest of the flour gradually until a smooth not sticky dough is formed, about 10 minutes.

Set the dough aside, cover with a wet cloth or wrap in plastic wrap, and begin preparing the filling.

To prepare the filling:

In a large skillet over medium heat, heat the oil, cumin seeds, and mustard seeds. The seeds will begin to pop. You may want to employ a lid to keep from getting hit with any popping seeds. Let them pop for about a minute, then add the onions and carrots. Raise the heat to medium-high and sauté for 7 to 10 minutes, till the onions begin to brown. Add the garlic, ginger, coriander, turmeric, cayenne, salt, and lemon juice, and sauté a minute more. Add the potatoes, mashing the potatoes with the spatula or a potato masher as you go along. When potatoes are mashed well and heated through, add the edamame and mix well.

Divide the dough in half and on a floured surface roll the dough out thinly. Now comes the fun part (or, the pain in the ass depending on your temperament). Let's form the little cutie pies. Have a small bowl of water ready. With a 4-inch cookie cutter (or something with a 4-inch circumference) cut out eight circles.

For small samosas:

Cut the dough circles in half, creating semi-circles. Gently pull the dough to stretch it a bit. With your fingertips, brush the cut edge with water, then fold it over, corner to corner, and seal along the straight edge with your thumb and forefinger. You should now have a cone. Stuff 1½ to 2 teaspoons of filling into the cone, then dab the open edges with water and again seal with your fingers. Repeat until you have thirty-six samosas.

For larger samosas:

Instead of slicing the dough circles in half, place 1½ tablespoons into the center of an entire circle, then dab the circumference with water, fold over the filling to form a pillowlike semicircle, and seal with your thumb and forefinger.

To bake:

Brush each side of the samosas lightly with oil and place on a baking sheet that has been sprayed with nonstick cooking spray or very lightly brushed with oil. For large samosas: Bake for 15 minutes. Flip the samosas over, bake for 10 more minutes, or until lightly browned. For small samosas: Bake for 12 minutes, flip over and bake for 8 minutes, or until lightly browned. I like to let them sit for at

VEGAN WITH A VENGEANCE

least 5 minutes, to let the crust flake just right. These freeze well; to reheat bake small ones at 350 for 20 minutes, larger ones for 25 to 30 minutes.

PUNK POiNTS

To make frozen peas taste like peas and not like freezer, run them under cool water to remove the icy freezer stuff, then drain.

Coconut–Mint Chutney

½ cup coconut milk
⅓ cup finely chopped fresh mint
⅓ cup finely chopped fresh coriander
1 clove garlic, minced
1 teaspoon pure maple syrup
1 teaspoon fresh lime juice
¼ teaspoon salt

Mix together all the ingredients in a medium-size bowl and refrigerate for 1 hour. Serve at room temperature.

LITTLE MEALS, SAMMICHES, AND FINGER FOODS

VEGAN WITH A VENGEANCE

Black Bean, Mushroom, and Quinoa-Stuffed Peppers

Again, this is a recipe inspired by my mom. She's been making stuffed peppers for years from a recipe off of a veggie crumbles package. She bugged me pretty much daily to put this recipe in the cookbook and I had to remind her, "Mom, no prepackaged foods, for the love of God!" One day she came over armed with the recipe and was determined to somehow force it into the cookbook. We came up with this recipe instead, and now everyone is happy.

2 tablespoons olive oil
1 medium-size onion, finely chopped (about 1 cup)
3 cloves garlic, minced
2 cups finely chopped mushrooms
1 tablespoon chile powder
1 teaspoon salt
1 (15-ounce) can tomato sauce
¼ cup water
½ cup quinoa
4 large red bell peppers
1 (15-ounce) can black beans, drained and rinsed
1 teaspoon pure maple syrup
Fresh cilantro for garnish

In a saucepan over medium heat, sauté the onions in the olive oil for 3 to 5 minutes, until the onions are translucent. Add the garlic and mushrooms; sauté about 5 minutes, until the mushrooms have released their moisture. Stir in the chile powder and salt. Add the quinoa and 1 cup of the tomato sauce (reserve the rest) and the water, lower the heat and cover, and simmer for about 20 minutes, stirring once.

Meanwhile, preheat the oven to 350°F and prepare the peppers: Boil a pot of water. Cut the tops off the peppers and remove the seeds. Boil the peppers for 5 minutes and then drain them.

Combine the beans and maple syrup with the cooked quinoa mixture. Stuff each pepper with filling and stand them upright in a baking dish. Pour the remaining tomato sauce over the peppers and bake for 15 minutes. Remove from oven, garnish with cilantro, and serve.

Fresh Mango Summer Rolls

Crisp vegetables and sweet mango make these the perfect treat for a hot summer's night, when the last thing you want to do is turn on the oven. The noodles are the only things that require cooking, and they're done in 10 minutes. You should be able to find rice noodles and wrappers in the ethnic foods section of a well-stocked supermarket, at a health food store, or at an Asian grocery. My sister supplied me with the dipping sauce recipe; I'm not sure where she got the recipe so if she "borrowed" it from you, I apologize in advance.

> 1 mango, peeled and sliced into matchsticks (see Punk Points, page 154)
> 1 cup bean sprouts, or seedless cucumber, sliced into matchsticks
> ½ cup fresh cilantro leaves
> 4 ounces very thin rice noodles
> ¼ cup roasted peanuts, very finely chopped
> 20 rice paper wrappers (plus extra in case some tear)
> Thai Dipping Sauce (recipe follows)

Boil a medium-size pot of water. Turn off the heat and add the noodles. Let them soak for 10 minutes, stirring occasionally. Drain the noodles and run them under cold water until they feel cold. Transfer them to a bowl and begin your rolls.

Have ready a pie pan or large wide bowl filled with hot water (tap water is fine) and clean counter space or a cutting board. Place the rice paper wrappers, two at a time, into the water until they are flexible (30 seconds to a minute). Carefully remove from water and lay flat on a clean surface. In the lower two-thirds of the roll, place a tablespoon of noodles and sprinkle a few of the chopped peanuts (about ½ a teaspoon) over them. On top of that place five or six mango strips and on top of that place six or seven bean sprouts and three or four cilantro leaves. Fold the left and right sides over the filling, then take the bottom of the wrapper and begin rolling. It may take a couple of tries to get it right, but keep it up and you're on your way to summer roll heaven. Keep wrapped and chilled until ready to eat and serve with small fingerbowls of the dipping sauce below.

VEGAN WITH A VENGEANCE

Thai Dipping Sauce

¼ cup rice vinegar

¼ cup water

1 teaspoon Asian chile oil

1 garlic clove, minced

3 tablespoons roasted peanuts, chopped

1½ teaspoons sugar

Mix all the ingredients together and chill until ready to serve.

Seitan- and Herb-Stuffed Mushrooms

These make great hors d'oeuvres or appetizers to an Italian meal. They are very omnifriendly so don't hesitate to serve them to your Uncle Ted who still thinks that passing you turkey at Thanksgiving is the funniest joke ever.

⅓ cup walnuts
30 large (about 2 inches in diameter) white mushrooms (about 1½ pounds), wiped clean
½ cup seitan, diced as small as you can make it
3 tablespoons olive oil
1 small onion, very finely chopped (1 cup)
2 cloves garlic, minced
¼ teaspoon dried thyme
¼ teaspoon dried basil
¼ teaspoon dried oregano
½ teaspoon salt
Several dashes fresh black pepper
¼ cup chopped fresh parsley
1 teaspoon finely grated lemon zest
Juice of 1 lemon
¾ cups plain bread crumbs

Preheat oven to 375°F.

Toast the walnuts: Heat a large skillet over medium heat. Place the walnuts in the pan and toast for 3 minutes, turning frequently. Remove from heat and let cool. Chop coarsely and set aside.

Remove the stems from the mushrooms. Set the stems aside. Place the mushrooms in a lightly greased baking pan, stem side down, and bake for 10 minutes. Remove from oven. When cool enough, drain the liquid that was released by the mushrooms. While they are cooling, prepare the stuffing.

Finely chop the mushroom stems. Heat a large skillet over medium-high. Sauté the stems and seitan in the olive oil for about 5 minutes. Add the onion, garlic, dried spices, and salt and pepper, and sauté for 5 more minutes. Add the parsley,

VEGAN WITH A VENGEANCE

lemon zest, and lemon juice, and mix well. Cook for 3 more minutes. In a large bowl, combine the vegetable mixture, bread crumbs, and toasted walnuts. Use your hands to mix well. If mixture is too dry, add the reserved mushroom cooking liquid by the tablespoonful until the mixture holds together when pinched.

Mound the filling into the mushroom caps, gently pressing it in. Bake filling side up on a baking pan for 20 minutes.

VEGAN WITH A VENGEANCE

Black-eyed Pea and Quinoa Croquettes with Mushroom Sauce

Quinoa is hands-down my favorite grain (even if it isn't technically a grain). Since it is a prerequisite for every vegetarian cookbook to tell you this, you probably know it is a complete protein. All too often it's made into a salad or thrown willy-nilly under a stir-fry. I wanted to give it the treatment in the form of these cute, savory croquettes. Serve with extra quinoa and Mushroom Sauce.

1½ cups cooked black-eyed peas, drained, or 1 (15-ounce) can, drained and rinsed
1 tablespoon olive oil
1 tablespoon soy sauce
1 cup cooked quinoa, at room temperature
½ teaspoon dried thyme, crumbled
½ teaspoon dried basil, crumbled
1 teaspoon paprika

FOR THE BREAD CRUMB COATING:
½ cup bread crumbs (I prefer whole wheat)
⅛ teaspoon salt
A few dashes fresh black pepper
½ teaspoon finely grated lemon zest
2 teaspoons olive oil

Preheat the oven to 350°F.

In a mixing bowl mash the black-eyed peas with a potato masher and then with your hands. Add the olive oil and soy sauce and stir. Add the quinoa and spices and combine the mixture with your hands. You should be able to mold them into balls that readily stick together.

In a small bowl mix together all the ingredients for the breading. Spray a baking pan with a little oil. Form the croquettes into walnut-sized ball. Gently roll the balls between your palms three or four times, then flatten out the ends so that the croquettes resemble marshmallows. Coat each ball with the bread crumbs and place on the prepared baking sheet. When all the croquettes have been formed, spray lightly with oil. Bake for 40 minutes, turning once after 20 minutes.

VEGAN WITH A VENGEANCE

I serve these by putting some cooked quinoa into the center of the plate, then putting four croquettes around the quinoa, then putting a healthy dose of mushroom sauce on the quinoa. Don't pour the sauce directly on the croquettes or they will get mushy.

Fizzle says:

1 cup of quinoa contains more calcium than a quart of milk.

Mushroom Sauce

This makes a *great pasta sauce as well, to make it more of a gravy add 1/4 cup flour to the broth and arrowroot mixture.*

3 cups vegetable broth
2 tablespoons arrowroot powder
1 tablespoon olive oil
1 small onion, finely chopped
2 cloves garlic, minced
2 cups crimini mushrooms, thinly sliced
1 teaspoon dried thyme
1 teaspoon salt
a few dashes fresh black pepper
1/2 cup white cooking wine
3 tablespoons soy sauce
1/4 cup nutritional yeast flakes
1/4 cup plain soy milk

In a small bowl whisk the arrowroot into vegetable broth until dissolved. Set aside.

In a medium sauce pan sauté the onions and garlic in the olive oil for 3 minutes. Add the mushrooms, thyme, salt and pepper and cook for 5 minutes, stirring occasionally. Add the white wine and turn the heat up high to bring to a boil for 3 minutes. Add the soy sauce and the broth/arrowroot mixture. Bring to a boil and then lower heat and simmer for 15 minutes, stirring occasionally. Add the nutritional yeast and whisk until dissolved. Add the soy milk and whisk for another minute or so. Let cool for a few minutes before serving.

VEGAN WITH A VENGEANCE

Parsnip-Scallion Pancakes

The fresh, slightly sweet taste of parsnips doesn't need too much spicing up; the green onions add just enough subtle bite.

> 4 cups shredded, peeled parsnips
> 1 cup finely chopped scallions
> ½ cup all-purpose flour
> 2 teaspoons canola oil plus extra for frying
> ½ teaspoon salt
> A few dashes fresh black pepper
> ⅓ to ½ cup water

Combine the parsnips and scallions in a large mixing bowl, mixing to evenly distribute the scallions. Add the flour, oil, salt, and pepper, tossing to coat. Add ⅓ cup of water and mix until the batter holds together when given a squeeze. Add a little more water if necessary.

Preheat a heavy-bottomed skillet over medium-high heat. Add about ¼ inch of oil. To test if the pan is ready, throw in a little pinch of the batter; if bubbles form around it immediately, it is ready. Form about 2 tablespoons of batter into a ball, then flatten out into a disk about 2 inches wide. Add the pancake to the oil, and continue with the rest of the batter, without crowding, cooking each pancake for 2½ to 3 minutes on each side, until golden brown. Note: I usually make a batch of eight, by the time the eighth is placed in the pan, the first pancake that I put in is ready to be flipped. You may need to add extra oil when you make the second batch.

When pancakes are done, transfer to a paper bag to drain the oil.

Spanakopita (Spinach Pies)

My friend Terry brings us this awesome recipe that I have enjoyed at many a potluck. She offers us three different ways to make it: a simple triangle shape, a wacky spiral, and a layered pie in a casserole dish. Skeptics take note: Terry's boyfriend is Greek so these pies have been under much scrutiny and they have passed the test.

¼ cup plus 2 tablespoons olive oil, plus extra oil for brushing the phyllo
2 bunches fresh spinach, rinsed very well, long stems removed
1 bunch scallions, trimmed and finely chopped
3 cloves garlic, minced
1 cup chopped dill
2 pounds firm tofu, drained and pressed
⅓ cup fresh lemon juice
2 teaspoons dried oregano
Dash of ground or freshly grated nutmeg
¾ cup finely ground walnuts
¼ cup nutritional yeast
1 teaspoon salt
Several dashes fresh ground black pepper
1 box frozen phyllo dough, thawed overnight

In a large heavy-bottomed pot warm 2 tablespoons of the olive oil over medium heat for a minute, then add the spinach, scallions, garlic, and dill. Add the spinach in small batches if pot is too full. Sauté till completely wilted and soft and a good amount of liquid has sweated out of the greens. Remove from heat and set aside to cool to room temperature.

In a large separate bowl mash the drained tofu (use your hands for more control) to a smooth but slightly grainy consistency. Take the cooled spinach mixture by small handfuls and squeeze out as much liquid as humanly possible (discard the liquid); add the squeezed spinach to the tofu. Add the lemon juice, oregano, nutmeg, ground walnuts, ¼ cup of the olive oil, and the nutritional yeast. Mix well with your hands, season with salt and pepper. Taste the mixture; it should taste pleasantly salty and tangy. Make sure the filling has cooled to room temperature before stuffing into the phyllo dough as directed below.

Traditional triangle shape:

MAKES ABOUT THIRTY TRIANGLES

Preheat oven to 350°F. Take two sheets of dough; brushing olive oil generously onto one sheet, layer the second sheet on top, also brushing that sheet with oil. Score the stacked dough sheets lengthwise into three strips. With the short end of a strip nearest you, place a scant 2 tablespoons of filling toward the top left corner of the long rectangle. Grabbing the corner of the dough, fold it rightward so it forms a triangle, fold it toward the left to form another triangle, and continue folding in this manner (like folding a flag, try burning this . . .) till you just can't fold any more. Wrap any remaining bit of dough around, underneath the triangle. Brush with lots of olive oil and bake on a baking sheet for 10 to 12 minutes, till deep golden brown and puffy. These can burn easily, so watch it!.

Back-to-Athens coil shape:

MAKES ABOUT FIFTEEN ROUND SPANAKOPITA

Terry tells us: "I have no idea if Socrates would teach at the foot of a mountain of these back in ancient Greece . . . just that all the spanakopita I ate in Greece were shaped like these. They are basically cute snail-shaped buns. They never get as brown as the triangles and are a little less flaky but still yum."

Preheat oven to 375°F. Taking two sheets, brush with oil as for the triangles. Score the dough lengthwise into two strips. Run about 2 to 3 tablespoons of filling along one long edge of each piece. Carefully roll up the long strip, starting from the filling side, to form a long, thick rope o' spanakopita. Then, daintily roll up your coil to form a snail-shaped bun. Brush with lots of oil. Bake for about 25 minutes till golden brown on top and lightly browned on the bottom.

Easy as π shape:

SERVES 8

You have no time for horrible Greek jokes so this one's for you: a spinach pie casserole, neat square slices well suited for serving as an entrée with salad.

Preheat oven to 375°F. Prepare eight sheets of dough with olive oil as for the triangle shape. Oil a 9 × 12- to 13-inch baking dish and, place the dough layers inside, patting any extra dough up the sides of the pan. Gently spread the spinach mixture on top of the dough. Prepare another eight layers of phyllo (or add a few

VEGAN WITH A VENGEANCE

more layers if you have leftover dough), put on top of spinach layer, and tuck into the sides of the pan any overhanging dough.

Lightly score the top layer of dough into 8 rectangles of equal size (this will prevent the dough from crumbling too much when slicing after it's baked). Brush with lots of olive oil. Bake 35 to 40 minutes till golden brown, being careful not to let the phyllo burn.

Phyllo is full of surprises the first time you handle it. You can't expose it to air for more than a few seconds before it dries out and becomes completely useless, so have handy several damp, clean kitchen towels and some plastic wrap. Don't spaz out! It's easy once you get the hang of it, and you'll be making phyllo this and that all the time and soon your friends will have to plan some kind of intervention. To make your life easier, make sure you have plenty of workspace on a clean, smooth surface. Since you'll be working with olive oil, have handy one of those pump mist sprayers that you can fill with any oil of choice. Or just have a bowl filled with olive oil and apply with a pastry brush.

VEGAN WITH A VENGEANCE

Cauliflower-Leek Kugel with Almond-Herb Crust

I was making this with my mom one Passover and she kept exclaiming how wonderful the dill smells and how I should be grateful that the Absolute has provided such an abundance of fresh leafy things. Then she went on and on about how I should join her philosophy school so I could learn to appreciate things. Then she asked me why I don't get laser surgery to remove my tattoos. You see, in Jewish culture, even something as simple as a great-smelling herb can lead to nagging. Fortunately she only had yums and mmms while we were eating. This recipe was inspired by one in Bon Appétit, veganized, modified, and vastly improved. If you eat tofu on Passover (some do, some don't) then it's Passover happy.

4 cups cauliflower florets (about 2 medium-size heads cauliflower)
3 whole matzohs
1 (12-ounce) package silken tofu
4 tablespoons olive oil
4 cups coarsely chopped leeks (white and green parts from about 2 leeks)
1 small onion, cut into ½-inch dice (about 1 cup)
½ cup chopped fresh parsley
½ cup chopped fresh dill
1½ teaspoons salt
½ teaspoon ground black pepper
½ cup almonds, toasted and chopped

Preheat oven to 350°F.

Boil a large pot of water. Add the cauliflower and cook for 10 minutes, covered. Meanwhile, prepare the matzoh mixture.

Crumble the two sheets of matzoh into a food processor or blender. Grind the matzoh into crumbs; remove from food processor and set aside. Crumble the tofu into the food processor or blender, and puree until smooth. You may have to add a couple of tablespoons of water. Let the tofu sit until you're ready to use it.

When the cauliflower is done, drain and transfer to a large bowl. Mash coarsely with a potato masher.

Heat 2 tablespoons of the oil in a large skillet over medium-high heat. Add the leeks and onions; sauté until the leeks are tender and the onions are translucent, about 5 minutes. Add to the cauliflower. Mix in the matzoh crumbs. Add the pureed tofu, 1

VEGAN WITH A VENGEANCE

tablespoon of the parsley, 1 tablespoon of the dill, salt, and pepper, and mix well.

Brush or spray a 9 × 13-inch casserole dish with oil. Spread the cauliflower mixture evenly in the dish. Mix together the almonds and remaining herbs. Crumble the remaining matzoh into large crumbs with your fingers and add the remaining 2 tablespoons of olive oil to them; mix. Sprinkle this mixture evenly over the kugel.

Bake for 35 minutes, until browned on top. Remove from oven and let stand for 10 minutes.

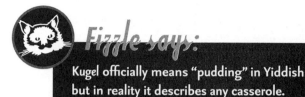

Fizzle says:

Kugel officially means "pudding" in Yiddish but in reality it describes any casserole.

LITTLE MEALS, SAMMICHES AND FINGER FOODS

VEGAN WITH A VENGEANCE

Chickpea Broccoli Casserole

This is a nice healthy veggie-ful meal, especially if you're feeling lazy, since all the ingredients go into one pan. After the prep work you bake it for an hour, while you kick back and pay the bills or update your blog. It is a little bland, but not in a bad way, since sometimes you just want the comforting taste of veggies without all those pesky spices. I would suggest making it this way once just to see that it is possible to make an eggless, cheeseless casserole and then doctor it with fresh herbs and spices some other time. I, however, love it just as is.

3 (16-ounce) cans chickpeas, drained and rinsed (or equivalent amount cooked
    chickpeas)
1 large onion, quartered and thinly sliced
3 large carrots, grated (about 2 cups)
1 head broccoli, cut into small florets (about 4 cups)
2 tablespoons thinly sliced chives
½ cup bread crumbs (preferably whole wheat)
3 tablespoons olive oil
1 cup vegetable broth
1 teaspoon salt

Preheat oven to 350°F

In a large bowl mash the chickpeas well, using a potato masher or a firm fork; it takes about 2 minutes to get the right consistency. Add the vegetables and mix well. Add the bread crumbs and mix, then add the oil and mix again. Finally, add the vegetable broth and salt, and mix one last time. Transfer all ingredients to a 9 × 13-inch (preferably glass or ceramic) casserole dish. Press the mixture firmly into the casserole. Cover with foil, bake for 45 minutes. Uncover and bake for 15 more minutes. Serve it hot the day of, but it tastes good cold as well.

LITTLE MEALS, SAMMICHES, AND FINGER FOODS

VEGAN WITH A VENGEANCE

Your Kitchen Wall: Structurally important Object Holding up Your Roof *or* Storage Facility?

I am by no means an organized person. My brother-in-law likes to say I "don't believe in dresser drawers" because of the abundance of clothing on my bedroom floor. When it comes to my kitchen, however, I need things to be relatively organized or I know that it will only take that much longer to eat.

My method for organizing is basically this: Have as much hanging on the walls as possible. You can usually buy hanging devices relatively cheaply at most hardware stores, but if you aren't looking for anything fancy you can pound some long nails into a long piece of strong wood and hang that up. I keep all of my pots, strainers, and most of my utensils on the wall, freeing up tons of valuable cabinet and shelf space. The other thing that's great about hanging pots and pans is that you won't fill up your dish drainer; you can simply hang them up to dry.

Falafel

If you attended Jewish day camp you might have grown up thinking that Judaism was a series of humiliating acts wherein you had to don curious things on your head and wear brightly colored face paint and then dance around in the hot sun while lethargic adults looked on. Case in point: One summer, my fellow campers and I dressed up as falafel and sang a song to the tune of the Kinks "Come Dancing." It went "Fa-la-fel . . . I like to eat it on a Saturday; fa-la-fel . . . the taste is natural." Somehow I came out of all this still loving falafel to pieces. If you don't have a food processor, you can still make it by chopping the onions, garlic, and parsley as finely as possible and then mashing everything really, really, really well.

2 cups cooked chickpeas, drained, or canned chickpeas, drained and rinsed
¼ cup whole wheat bread crumbs
2 tablespoons all-purpose flour
1 medium-size onion, chopped
2 cloves garlic, chopped
½ teaspoon baking powder
1 teaspoon ground cumin
1 teaspoon ground coriander
¼ teaspoon cayenne pepper
¼ cup chopped fresh flat-leaf parsley
½ teaspoon salt
A few dashes fresh black pepper
Vegetable oil for frying
4 large pita breads, sliced in half to make 2 pockets apiece
Lettuce
Chopped tomato, red onion, and cucumber
Tahini Dressing (page 121)

In a food processor combine the chickpeas and bread crumbs; pulse for about 30 seconds until the chickpeas are chopped. Add the remaining ingredients (through the black pepper) and process, scraping down the sides, until relatively smooth but somewhat coarse. The mixture should look fairly green from the parsley. Transfer to a bowl, cover, and refrigerate for at least ½ hour.

Shape the batter into 1½-inch balls and then flatten into 2-inch-diameter patties. In a large heavy-bottomed pan (cast iron is ideal) heat about ½ inch of vegetable oil. Test the oil by throwing in a pinch of the batter; if the oil immediately bubbles up rapidly, it is ready. Cook the patties in the oil in two batches, 2½ to 3 minutes per

VEGAN WITH A VENGEANCE

side. Remove with a slotted spoon and transfer to a flattened paper bag or paper towels to drain.

Prepare the sammiches by stuffing the pita bread with falafel, lettuce, tomato, red onion, and cucumber, and drizzling in the tahini dressing.

VEGAN WITH A VENGEANCE

Curried Tempeh–Mango Salad Sammiches

I usually make a sammich out of these but it would be just as good over a salad with a little citrus dressing. Mangoes and tempeh are surprisingly compatible and the curry powder pulls everything together.

> 1 (8-ounce) package tempeh
> 1 tablespoon soy sauce
> 1 cup mango (less than 1 mango), peeled and chopped into ¼-inch chunks (see Punk Points, page 154)
> ¼ cup scallions, chopped

FOR THE DRESSING:
> 3 tablespoons Vegannaise
> 2 teaspoons curry powder
> Juice of 2 limes
> 2 tablespoons apple cider vinegar
> 1 teaspoon sugar
> ½ teaspoon hot sauce
> Pinch salt

FOR SAMMICHES:
> 2 large pitas, cut in half to make 2 pockets apiece
> Thinly sliced red onion
> Lettuce
> Extra mango slices

Tear the tempeh into bite-sized pieces and place in a small saucepan. Cover with water and add the soy sauce. Cover the pot and bring to a boil, then simmer for 15 minutes. Drain and transfer the tempeh to a bowl to cool.

Meanwhile, whisk together all the ingredients for the dressing.

Add the mangoes and scallions to the tempeh. Add the dressing; mix well. Cover and refrigerate for at least an hour and up to overnight, to allow flavors to meld. Adjust the seasonings as you see fit. Serve in pitas with lettuce, red onion, and extra mango slices.

Veggie Burgers

Textured vegetable protein (TVP) gives these burgers a meaty satisfying bite, plus it ensures that the burger won't fall apart like so many homemade veggie burgers tend to do. Serve on buns with all your favorite fixings (I'm a Vegannaise and pickles girl) and Sweet Potato Fries (page 114).

1 medium-size onion, finely chopped
½ cup finely chopped, peeled carrot
1 cup finely chopped mushrooms
2 cloves garlic, minced
2 tablespoons olive oil
1½ cups vegetable broth or water
3 tablespoons soy sauce
3 tablespoons tomato paste
1 cup textured vegetable protein
½ teaspoon dried thyme
½ teaspoon dried oregano
½ teaspoon dried paprika
2 teaspoons Dijon mustard
1 tablespoon peanut butter
¼ teaspoon liquid smoke (optional)
¼ cup oat flour
Oil for cooking

In a medium-size saucepan over moderate heat sauté the onions, carrot, mushrooms, and garlic in the olive oil for 7 minutes. Add the broth, soy sauce, tomato paste, vegetable protein, dried herbs, and paprika. Cover and bring to a boil, then lower heat and simmer about 7 minutes. Uncover and cook 3 to 5 minutes more, stirring occasionally, until the TVP is fully cooked and the texture is meaty.

Transfer to a mixing bowl and let cool just until it is cool enough to handle (about 5 minutes). Add the mustard, peanut butter, and liquid smoke (if using); mix well. Add the oat flour and mix again. Cover and refrigerate for at least half an hour.

Using about ¼ cup of the mix, roll into balls. Shape into burgers 2½ to 3 inches wide. Preheat a large, preferably nonstick skillet and pour in a very thin layer of oil (2 tablespoons should do it). When the oil is hot, add the veggie burgers and cook for about 5 minutes on each side; they should be nicely browned and firm to the touch. Serve with all your favorite burger fixings.

LITTLE MEALS, SAMMICHES AND FINGER FOODS

VEGAN WITH A VENGEANCE

Tempeh Reuben

If I haven't told you enough times, I was practically raised in a Jewish deli. I especially loved big Reubens filled with plenty of sauerkraut, Thousand Island dressing, and the non-traditional pickle. I do get a little misty eyed when I pass a deli and can't pay a visit to my lost love Reuben but sometimes he is waiting for me at home. I am not a big fan of soy cheese but if you are, feel free to add some shredded Swiss-style cheese.

8 slices good, dark pumpernickel bread

8 teaspoons nonhydrogenated margarine

1½ cups sauerkraut

2 dill pickles, thinly sliced

1 avocado, cut in half lengthwise and sliced into ¼-inch slices

1 pound tempeh, cut into four equal pieces, then cut through the middle so that you have eight thin squares

FOR THE MARINADE:

½ cup white cooking wine

2 tablespoons olive oil

2 tablespoons balsamic vinegar

2 tablespoons Bragg Liquid Aminos or tamari

2 tablespoon fresh lemon juice

2 cloves garlic, smashed

FOR THE DRESSING:

⅓ cup Vegannaise

2 tablespoons ketchup

Juice of 1 lemon

1 tablespoon minced onion

3 teaspoons capers

2 tablespoons sweet pickle relish (or equivalent amount chopped pickles)

A pinch of cayenne

Prepare the tempeh:

Combine all the ingredients for the marinade. Add the tempeh and marinate for at least an hour, turning once.

Mix together all the dressing ingredients and set aside.

When the tempeh has marinated for an hour, preheat a grill pan over high heat. Cook the slices on the grill for 4 minutes on one side, until dark grill lines have appeared, then use tongs to flip them over and cook on the other side for about 3 minutes.

Prepare the sammich:

Spread a teaspoon of margarine on each piece of bread. Heat a large skillet over moderate heat. Fry each piece of bread on the buttered side for 3 minutes, flip over and cook 1 minute more (it's okay that the other side is dry).

Divide the sammich ingredients equally among four buttered-side-down fried bread slices. Smother in dressing, top each serving with another slice of fried bread, nonbuttered side down, cut in half, and serve. For that authentic Jewish deli look, stick a toothpick in each half.

Fizzle says:

You can get canned, jarred, or bagged sauerkraut at the grocery store but for the best results ask the deli counter at your supermarket if they have any fresh sauerkraut.

VEGAN WITH A VENGEANCE

TLT (Tempeh, Lettuce, and Tomato)

Tempeh, bacon, and hummus (and lettuce and tomato)—absolutely delish.

> 8 slices sourdough bread, toasted
> 1 batch Tempeh Bacon (page 23)
> 1 cup hummus
> 1 large tomato, thinly sliced
> Thinly sliced red onion
> 4 leaves romaine lettuce
> 1 cup alfalfa sprouts

Layer one slice of bread with hummus; pile on the tempeh bacon, then the tomato, onion, lettuce, and sprouts. Add a dollop of hummus to keep the sammich intact, top with another slice of bread, slice in half, and serve. Repeat for the other three sammiches.

Tofu Dill Salad Sammiches

This combination of very simple ingredients produce a fresh-tasting salad that is perfect for those summer months when you just couldn't possibly cook.

1 pound extra-firm tofu, drained and pressed
3 tablespoons minced red onion
3 tablespoons Vegannaise
⅓ cup fresh dill, chopped
2 teaspoons Dijon mustard
2 tablespoons apple cider vinegar or fresh lemon juice
Salt and fresh black pepper to taste
8 slices whole wheat bread
Sammich fixings (lettuce, tomato, and onion)

In a large bowl, crumble the tofu with your hands for about 30 seconds, until you reach a crumbly but still somewhat firm consistency. Add the rest of the ingredients through the pepper, chill for about 15 minutes. Serve on whole wheat bread spread with a little extra Vegannaise and topped with lettuce, tomato, and onion.

VEGAN WITH A VENGEANCE

Chickpea-Hijiki Salad Sammiches

Okay you got me, I miss tuna fish sandwiches. These sammiches satisfy my craving, and if you haven't cooked with hijiki before don't be intimidated—the taste is not incredibly fishy, especially in such a small quantity.

> 1 tablespoon dried hijiki
> Boiling water
> 1 (15-ounce) can chickpeas, drained
> 3 tablespoons Vegannaise
> 2 tablespoons apple cider vinegar
> 2 tablespoons minced onion
> ½ cup peeled, shredded carrot
> Salt and fresh black pepper to taste
> Sammich fixings (lettuce, tomato, and onion)
> 8 slices whole wheat bread, toasted

Place the hijiki in a small bowl and poor boiling water over it to cover. Cover the bowl with a plate and let the hijiki sit for about 15 minutes. Meanwhile, prepare the rest of the ingredients.

In a large bowl mash the chickpeas with a potato masher until no whole beans are left. Add the remaining ingredients and mix well. When the hijiki is ready, drain and combine it with the chickpea mixture. Refrigerate for at least 15 minutes; serve on toasted whole wheat with lettuce, tomato, and onion.

Fizzle says:

Hijiki, like other seaweeds, is a rich source of iron, protein, calcium, zinc, and iodine.

LITTLE MEALS, SAMMICHES, AND FINGER FOODS

VEGAN WITH A VENGEANCE

I admit I don't get too fussy when it comes to side dishes, so all of these recipes are fairly simple. The most valuable thing about this chapter, though, is the methods, because once you master several cooking methods you can throw away all your cookbooks (except this one) and start a cooking revolution. So prepare to roast, bake, braise, and blanch, and we'll cook a little rice while we're at it.

SIDES

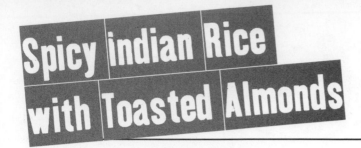

Spicy indian Rice with Toasted Almonds

I only do up my rice if I'm having friends over, otherwise plain basmati suits me just fine. But when I want to go the extra mile I make this to go with my curry. Frying the almonds intensifies the flavor and will have your guests wide eyed and asking what you did to the almonds to make them taste so good.

> 3 tablespoons vegetable oil
> ¼ cup slivered almonds
> 1 medium-size onion, cut into ½-inch dice
> 2 cloves garlic, minced
> 1 small serrano chile, seeded and finely chopped (or use jalapeño for less heat)
> 1 tablespoon minced fresh ginger
> 2 teaspoons cumin seeds
> ¼ teaspoon fennel seeds, crushed
> 2 cardamom pods
> 1 cinnamon stick
> ½ teaspoon salt
> 1½ cups basmati rice, washed and drained
> 2½ cups water
> ¼ cup raisins
> 1 carrot, grated

Heat the oil in a heavy-bottomed pot over moderate heat until hot but not smoking. Cook the almonds, stirring frequently, until golden, about 2 minutes. Transfer with a slotted spoon to paper towels to drain.

Add the onions to the pot and cook over medium-high heat for 5 to 7 minutes, until translucent. Add the garlic, chile, ginger, spices, and salt and sauté 1 minute more. Lower heat and add the rice. Cook for 5 minutes, stirring frequently. Add the water, bring to a boil, then lower heat. Simmer uncovered for about 5 minutes. Add the raisins, cover, and cook over very low heat for 20 more minutes. When most of the liquid has been absorbed, turn the heat off. Add the grated carrots and almonds, mix well, cover, and let sit for 10 more minutes. When the rice is done, fluff with a fork and serve.

VEGAN WITH A VENGEANCE

Coconut Rice with Toasted Coconut

This is an easy and tasty dish that looks pretty fancy with the toasted coconut on top. It's a perfect complement to BBQ Pomegranate Tofu (page 149) and it's also great with any Caribbean, Thai, or Indian dish.

> 2 cups jasmine rice, washed
> 1 (13.5-ounce) can coconut milk
> 1 cup water
> 1 cinnamon stick
> ¼ teaspoon salt
> Finely grated zest of 1 lime
> ½ cup unsweetened shredded coconut

Combine the rice, coconut milk, water, cinnamon stick, and salt in a saucepan and bring to a boil. Lower heat, cover pot, and simmer 20 minutes. Add the lime zest and stir with a fork. Remove from heat, cover, and let sit 10 more minutes. Meanwhile, prepare the shredded coconut:

Heat a skillet over low-medium heat. Add the coconut and toast, turning frequently, for about 3 minutes, or until the coconut is browned and toasty.

Remove the cinnamon stick from the rice and serve, sprinkling the toasted coconut over each serving. Garnish with lime wedges if you so desire.

Mashed Potatoes with Punk Rock Chickpea Gravy

So easy, so good. I usually use Yukon gold potatoes because they are thin-skinned but really any potato will work.

> 2 pounds potatoes, cut into 1-inch chunks
> 3 tablespoons nonhydrogenated margarine
> ½ cup unsweetened soy milk
> 1 teaspoon salt (or to taste)
> Several dashes fresh black pepper

Place the potatoes in a pot and cover with cold water. Cover and bring to a boil, then add some salt to the water. Re-cover and let boil for 20 minutes or so, until the potatoes are tender.

Drain the potatoes, then add back to the pot. Add the margarine, and mash with a potato masher. Add the soy milk and mash some more until the potatoes are fluffy-ish. Add the salt, black pepper, and more soy milk or margarine if you think the potatoes need it.

VARIATIONS

You can mix-and-match these flavor variations, if you like. For example, garlic-wasabi mashed potatoes are mighty yummy. Also, keep in mind that just about anything can be added to mashed potatoes: chives, curry powder, pesto . . . the possibilities are endless.

Garlic Mashed Potatoes: Sauté 4 to 6 cloves of minced garlic in 1½ tablespoons of olive oil and add to the potatoes when you add the margarine.

Wasabi Mashed Potatoes: Dissolve 1 tablespoon of wasabi powder in the soy milk before you add it.

Spinach Mashed Potatoes: Thaw a package of frozen spinach and pat it dry, or chop a bunch of spinach and sauté in water only until wilted; pat the spinach dry with a kitchen towel or paper towel. Add to potatoes at the end. (Spinach and garlic mashed potatoes are especially good.)

VEGAN WITH A VENGEANCE

Punk Rock Chickpea Gravy

MAKES ABOUT 3 CUPS

I feel like, if I had to reveal my soul via a gravy, then this would be it. Truth be told, I hate measuring and all that and am pretty good at eyeballing but you can't write a whole cookbook that depends on guessing the quantities. Still, you can have one recipe that breaks out, and this is it. I call it "punk rock" because it depends on almost every spice in your spice rack; it would make any "real" chef gasp. And every punk worth their weight in CRASS records knows that chickpeas are the punkest legume there is. Oh, it tastes crazy good, too. You will make it at least once a week. I just know it.

¼ cup all-purpose flour
Approximately 2½ cups water
1 tablespoon olive oil
1 medium-size onion, quartered and thinly sliced
2 teaspoons mustard seeds
3 cloves garlic, minced
2 cups cooked chickpeas, drained, or 1 (16-ounce) can, drained and rinsed
2 pinches of ground cumin
2 pinches of paprika
Pinch of dried rosemary
Pinch of dried thyme
Pinch of dried oregano
Pinch of ground coriander
3 tablespoons soy sauce
Juice of 1 lemon
¼ cup nutritional yeast

Mix the flour with 2 cups of water until the flour is mostly dissolved.

Heat a large skillet (preferably cast iron) over medium heat. Add the olive oil and let heat for 20 seconds or so. Add the onions and mustard seeds; cook for about 10 minutes, stirring occasionally, until the onions are browned and the mustard seeds are toasted. Add the garlic and sauté for 2 minutes more. Add the chickpeas; use a potato masher to mash them—you don't want to mash them into a paste, just make sure each one is broken up although if there are a few whole ones left that is okay. Add the herbs and spices, soy sauce, and lemon juice. Scrape the bottom of the pan to loosen any browned bits of onion.

Lower heat and pour the flour mixture into the pan. Stir constantly until a thick gravy forms. Stir in the nutritional yeast. If it looks too thick and pasty, add more water and mix well. It may look like it doesn't want any more water added to it, but just keep mixing and it will loosen up.

Keep warm until ready to serve.

VEGAN WITH A VENGEANCE

*I*n the late '90s I was feeling very isolated from any political community. I was working day and night to make ends meet. I even had three jobs: waitressing at two restaurants, and working at an organic produce warehouse. In my free time, I was either drinking or trying to write a novel that would never be finished.

I knew that I had to reconnect with my community—any progressive political community, really. My friend Amanda and I decided to start an anarcha-feminist potluck. The idea was this: every two weeks, get a bunch of hairy-legged women in a room together to share food, recipes, and politics. We would each bring a dish, eat, talk, and then have an informal roundtable where each woman would discuss where her political activism and interests lay. If you weren't politically active at the moment but wanted to be, you could say something like this: "My name is Eloise. I'm interested in prison reform work." Then someone, let's say Danielle, would say, "I'm active with Books Between Bars; let's talk after the meeting." And a prison reform activist would be born. We even had a little newsletter we passed out at meetings, called *Eat Me*, which listed events and happenings in the coming weeks. We also formed something called The Free(k) Economy, where each woman listed her skills, and whenever we needed help with something we could call on one another. It wasn't a barter system, rather a way for us to support one another in whatever way we were able to. I gave many haircuts and painted many rooms. Other women skill-shared: taught each other how to knit, weld, and even make homemade dildos!

Starting it was easy and this was before everyone and their Aunt Tilly had access to the Internet. We put up fliers in vegetarian restaurants, left-leaning bookstores, and colleges, and we also had a hotline number to call for information on the next potluck.

Some wonderful things came out of those potlucks, both culinary and politically. A lot of us helped to open a collective women's bookstore on the Lower East Side. We went to demonstrations together and hung anti-fascist fliers to telephone poles with wheat paste. And I'm not a big fan of street theater, but I have to admit that some embarrassing street performances did occur. I like to think that sharing food in one another's home helped us to work together and trust each other in a way that sitting around in a sterile church basement with fluorescent lighting might not have.

Maple-Mustard-Glazed Potatoes and String Beans

My best friend Erica is the kind of girl that throws a bunch of stuff together, pops it in the oven, forgets about it, goes to her sewing machine, makes a bag, remembers what's in the oven, takes it out, and it's delicious. These potatoes were always a hit at the potlucks, and when people asked for the recipe (and they always asked) she'd be like, "Potatoes, string beans, garlic, maple syrup, uhhhh, put it in the oven." Having lived with her for several years I was able to stage several psych ops through which I discerned this recipe.

2 pounds small Yukon gold potatoes, halved (about 1-inch pieces)
½ pound string beans, halved, ends cut off and discarded
1 yellow onion, thickly sliced
2 cloves garlic, minced
3 tablespoons tamari or soy sauce
¼ cup pure maple syrup
3 tablespoons Dijon mustard
2 tablespoons olive oil

Preheat oven to 400°F.

Place the vegetables in a 9 × 13-inch casserole dish. In a mixing bowl stir together all the other ingredients until the mustard is dissolved. Pour over the vegetables and mix well until everything is coated. Cover with foil and place in oven. Bake for 25 minutes. Remove from oven and toss everything; use a spoon to drip the sauce over the veggies. Turn oven down to 350°F, and cook for 25 minutes uncovered. Remove from oven, toss again, cook for 25 more minutes uncovered. These are especially yummy served at room temperature, with some of the remaining sauce poured over them.

VEGAN WITH A VENGEANCE

Sweet Potato Fries

This was one of the first recipes submitted to my site by Beth and it got positive reviews all around. Reviewers suggested other spices, such as sage or chile powder, so go ahead and be creative with your favorite spices. Even though sweet potatoes and yams are different, it is pretty common to use yams as you do sweet potatoes, so please don't get all technical on me; either one will work in this recipe.

> 2 large unpeeled sweet potatoes (about 2 pounds), cleaned and cut into ¼-inch strips lengthwise
> 1 tablespoon olive oil
> 1 teaspoon ground cumin
> 1 teaspoon ground coriander
> ¼ teaspoon black pepper

Preheat oven to 425°F. Lightly grease a large rimmed baking sheet.

Combine oil, cumin, coriander, and pepper in a large mixing bowl. Add the potatoes and toss well to coat. Arrange in a single layer on the prepared baking sheet. Bake for 15 minutes. Use tongs to flip potatoes over, and bake for another 10 to 15 minutes until browned.

"FRONCH" TOAST WITH TEMPEH BACON

(page 28 and 23)

LEMON CORN WAFFLES WITH BLUEBERRY SAUCE

(page 39)

MATZOH BALL SOUP
(page 70)

**SPANAKOPITA
(SPINACH PIE)**
(page 91)

FRESH MANGO
SUMMER ROLLS

(page 84)

MUSHROOM AND SUN-DRiED TOMATO RiSOTTO

(page 186)

ISA PiZZA

(page 131)

GREEN THAI CURRY

(page 172)

FAUSTESS CUPCAKES

(page 229)

LEMON GEM CUPCAKES

(page 228)

GINGER-MACADAMIA-
COCONUT-CARROT CAKE

(page 215)

Baked Cajun French Fries

Nice spicy fries that are baked, not fried. These taste great with any sammich, or by themselves when you're craving a savory snack. Okay, fine, I guess I don't need to tell you what to do with French fries.

4 large unpeeled russet potatoes, cleaned and cut lengthwise into ¼-inch strips
2 tablespoons olive oil
¾ teaspoon paprika
½ teaspoon ground cumin
¼ teaspoon dried oregano
¼ teaspoon dried thyme
¼ teaspoon cayenne
½ teaspoon coarse sea salt

Preheat oven to 450°F. Very lightly grease a large rimmed baking sheet.

In a mixing bowl toss the potatoes with the olive oil to coat. Mix the spices and salt together and toss with the potatoes to coat. It's okay if the mixture isn't coating every part of each potato; as long as there is some of the spice on each one, you're good.

Arrange the potatoes in a single layer on the prepared baking sheet; if they don't all fit use a second sheet. Bake for 20 minutes. Use tongs to flip the potatoes, bake for another 12 to 15 minutes. The fries should be golden brown. Serve immediately.

VEGAN WITH VENGEANCE

Ginger Roasted Winter Vegetables

Serve these sweet roasted veggies with garlicky greens and Grilled Tofu (page 145). They are beautiful to behold and the textures and flavors of the peppery parsnips, the sweetness of the squash, the gingeriness of the ginger, will send you into sensory overload.

> 1 pound parsnips (about 2 average-size), washed, peeled, and cut into ¾-inch chunks
>
> 2 large carrots, washed, peeled cut into ½-inch chunks
>
> 1 butternut squash, peeled, seeded, and cut into ¾-inch chunks
>
> 1 pound sweet potatoes (about 3 medium-size), peeled and cut into ¾-inch chunks
>
> 2 heaping tablespoons grated fresh ginger
>
> ¼ cup pure maple syrup
>
> ⅓ cup olive oil
>
> Pinch cinnamon
>
> Pinch allspice
>
> 1 teaspoon salt

Preheat oven to 350°F.

In a large bowl combine all ingredients, making sure all veggies are well coated. Doing this with your hands works best.

Place the veggies in a single layer on a rimmed baking sheet. If they don't all fit you may need to use two baking pans and rotate the pans halfway through baking. If there is any extra liquid, pour it over the veggies.

Bake for 25 minutes. Remove from oven and flip the veggies. Bake for 20 or so more minutes, until the veggies are tender inside.

Orange-Glazed Beets

The sweetness of the beets is heightened with this simple, tangy orange glaze. Serve this with Roasted Vegetables (see preceding recipe), Grilled Tofu (page 145) and a grain. They're also really yummy if you chill and use them in a salad.

1½ pounds beets (3 to 4 average-size), peeled, quartered, and sliced about ¼-inch thick
1 cup freshly squeezed orange juice
1 teaspoon finely grated orange zest
1 teaspoon pure maple syrup
1 teaspoon salt

Place all the ingredients in a large pan, cover, and bring to a low boil. Simmer, stirring occasionally, for about 12 minutes, or until the beets are tender. Uncover and boil until the liquid has reduced to a glaze, about 4 minutes more. These taste good hot, at room temperature, or chilled.

VEGAN WITH VENGEANCE

Braised Cauliflower with Three-Seed Sauce

Braising is basically sautéing and then steaming in its sauce, and cauliflower takes very well to it-it stays firm yet tender. This makes a nice side for any Indian-style meal; you can even make it an entrée and serve over basmati rice or with Spicy Indian Rice (page 108) if you like.

1 (28-ounce) can tomatoes, in juice
1 large onion, finely chopped (about 2 cups)
3 tablespoons olive oil
3 cloves garlic, minced
2 jalapeño peppers, stemmed, seeded and thinly sliced
¼ teaspoon salt
2 teaspoons cumin seeds
2 teaspoons mustard seed
1 teaspoon fennel seeds
½ teaspoon ground turmeric
1 bay leaf
1 head cauliflower, cut into large florets
½ teaspoon sugar

Remove the tomatoes from their juice; scoop the seeds out of the tomatoes with your fingers. Chop the tomatoes into quarters and set aside. Reserve the juice from the can.

In a large skillet over medium heat, sauté the onion in the olive oil for 10 minutes. Add the garlic, jalapeños, salt, seeds and spices, and the bay leaf; sauté for a minute. Add the cauliflower and sauté for 2 minutes. Add the sugar and tomatoes and cook for a minute. Add ½ cup of reserved tomato juice. Stir everything up, cover the pan, and let cook for 5 minutes, stirring occasionally. Uncover and cook for 5 more minutes, until the sauce thickens a bit and thecauliflower is tender but not mushy. Remove the bay leaf. This tastes best if you let it sit for about 15 minutes before serving.

VEGAN WITH A VENGEANCE

Balsamic-Glazed Portobello Mushrooms

A splash of vinegar enhances these mushrooms to heavenly heights. Garlic adds punch. The beauty is in the simplicity. Be careful not to overcook.

3 medium-size portobello caps, sliced ¼ inch thick
1 tablespoon olive oil
¼ cup balsamic vinegar
Pinch salt
2 cloves garlic, finely minced

Preheat a large skillet over medium-high heat for about 2 minutes.

Toss the mushrooms with the olive oil until coated. Place in pan in a single layer. Let cook for 5 minutes, until they start releasing moisture. Turn over and cook another 2 minutes.

Add the vinegar and salt; sauté for 30 seconds. Add the garlic and sauté for 3 more minutes. Tastes great warm, at room temperature, or chilled and used in a salad or sammich.

PUNK POINTS

To get the garlic as thin as possible use a straight razor blade to slice it. Not only will you get really nice even slices but you will feel cool as hell doing it.

VEGAN WITH A VENGEANCE

Garlicky Kale with Tahini Dressing

I love me some greens. You can prepare the kale without the dressing and serve it with . . . well, anything, really. I like to mash it into my mashed potatoes.

> 5 or 6 cloves garlic, thinly sliced
> 3 tablespoons olive oil
> 1 bunch kale, well rinsed and coarsely chopped
> ¼ teaspoon salt
> Tahini Dressing (recipe follows)
> Lemon wedges to serve

Sauté the garlic in olive oil over medium-high heat for about 2 minutes, stirring frequently, until golden brown. Add the kale and a few splashes of water. Use tongs to toss the kale around, coating it with the garlic and oil. Stir frequently for 4 to 5 minutes.

Serve with a drizzle of Tahini Dressing. I like to use a squeeze bottle for this but if you don't have one just use a spoon. Garnish with lemon wedges.

Fizzle says:

You can use the stems of the kale if they are on the thin side, about ¼ inch wide. If they are larger, cut the leaves from the stem.

VEGAN WITH A VENGEANCE

Tahini Dressing

MAKES 2 CUPS

This is way more than you need for the recipe above but I figure if you are making it might as well have some left over for salad and sammiches or falafel throughout the week. It is really important that you don't burn the garlic; you really just want to heat it and get the flavor into the oil.

8 teaspoons olive oil
3 cloves garlic, chopped
½ cup tahini
2 teaspoons balsamic vinegar
½ tsp salt
Juice of 1 lemon
Several dashes fresh black pepper
½ teaspoon paprika
¼ cup lightly packed fresh parsley
½ cup cold water

Heat the garlic in 6 teaspoons of the olive oil in a small sauté pan over very low heat for 2 minutes, just until it's fragrant.

Place the heated garlic and all the other ingredients except the parsley in the food processor or blender, and blend until smooth. Add the parsley and pulse until the parsley is very finely chopped but not pureed.

Refrigerate at least ½ hour in an airtight container. You may need to mix in a little extra water once it's chilled.

VEGAN WITH VENGEANCE

Roasted Applesauce

This is a standard Passover dish for me to bring as an alternative to that tiresome applesauce from a jar. Serve it alongside potato pancakes or Horseradish- and Coriander-Crusted Tofu (page 151) or any time you think, "This is good but it could use some applesauce."

3 pounds McIntosh apples (about 10 apples)
Juice of 1 lemon
2 tablespoons canola oil
¼ cup pure maple syrup
2 tablespoons sugar
1 teaspoon ground cinnamon
½ teaspoon finely grated lemon zest
Pinch ground allspice
¼ teaspoon salt

Preheat oven to 400°F.

Peel, core, and slice the apples into 1-inch chunks. Sprinkle with the lemon juice and set aside.

Combine the oil, maple syrup, sugar, cinnamon, and zest in a glass baking dish, and whisk together. Add the apples and toss to coat.

Roast until the apples are very tender, about 25 minutes, turning once after 15 minutes. Transfer to a large bowl and mash. If you prefer a smoother applesauce, you can pulse it a few times in a blender or food processor. You can serve this warm, at room temperature, or chilled.

Sautéed Green Beans with Mushrooms

Garlicky green beans and earthy mushrooms together at last. This is a great Thanksgiving dish or as a side to any Italian meal.

> 1 tablespoon olive oil
> 3 cloves garlic, finely chopped
> 1½ cups sliced cremini mushrooms
> ½ teaspoon dried oregano
> 4 teaspoons salt
> a few dashes fresh black pepper
> ½ cup vegetable broth or water
> ½ cup white cooking wine
> 2½ cups green beans, cut into 1-inch pieces

In a large nonstick pan over medium heat sauté the garlic in the olive oil for about 2 minutes, stirring frequently. Add mushrooms, oregano, salt, and pepper, and sauté until the mushrooms begin to release moisture, about 2 minutes. Add the vegetable broth and turn the heat up a bit, bringing to a low boil. Simmer for about a minute.

Add the white wine and green beans; cover and simmer for about 2 minutes. Uncover and cook for about 3 more minutes or until desired tenderness is reached.

VEGAN WITH VENGEANCE

Sesame Asparagus

Serve alongside the Asian Grilled Tofu (page 145) or any Asian type meal.

- 2 cloves garlic, minced
- 1 tablespoon toasted sesame oil
- 2 tablespoons soy sauce
- 2 tablespoons rice vinegar
- 1 teaspoon red pepper flakes
- 1 pound asparagus, ends discarded
- 2 tablespoons toasted sesame seeds

Sauté the garlic in the sesame oil over medium heat for about a minute. Add the soy sauce, vinegar, and red pepper flakes. Add the asparagus and sauté for 4 to 5 minutes, until the asparagus is still bright green and firm but slightly tender. Move to a serving plate and sprinkle with sesame seeds.

Roasted Brussels Sprouts with Toasted Garlic

Believe me when I tell you that these are amazing. No, seriously. Roasting the Brussels sprouts gives them a popcorn-y flavor. Gone are the days of overboiled Brussels sprouts covered in processed cheese; this is seriously good food.

    1 pound Brussels sprouts, washed and halved
    1 tablespoon olive oil
    3 cloves garlic, chopped
    ¼ teaspoon coarse sea salt

Preheat oven to 400°F.

Lay the Brussels sprouts on a rimmed baking sheet; douse with the olive oil. Roast for 10 minutes. Remove from oven, add the chopped garlic, and sprinkle with coarse sea salt, using tongs and toss to coat. Return to oven, roast for 5 more minutes. Before you remove the Brussels sprouts from the pan, rub them into the garlic, and, when you serve them, sprinkle with whatever toasted garlic remains in the pan.

VEGAN WITH A VENGEANCE

Pizza is the most social food there is. As each pie comes out of the oven, anticipation builds as you wait for it to cool just enough to slice it. The crowds gather ready to pounce and fight for their slice if need be. And then everyone sits around eating and saying, "Great pizza!" and coming up with topping ideas for the next one. Or just letting you do all the work. I put pastas here, too, to have a little Italian celebration, and because the sauces can perform double duty as pasta sauces.

PIZZAS AND PASTAS

Pizza Dough—A Novel

1 cup warm water
1½ tablespoons sugar
1 (¼-ounce) package active dry yeast*
2 tablespoons olive oil, plus about 2 teaspoons for the rising bowl
3 cups all-purpose flour
1 teaspoon salt
Cornmeal

* Not that rapid-rise stuff

The first step is to "proof" your yeast. I've been told that with modern yeast technology this step is unnecessary, but my mother-in-law does it, so I will, too. Pour the water (be sure it is warm, not hot) into a small bowl and dissolve the sugar in it, then add the yeast. Stir it a little bit so the yeast gets wet, and let it sit in a warm place for 10 minutes or so. When you come back it should be kind of foamy and maybe even bubbling a bit; if it is, congratulations! Your yeast is alive. If nothing's happened you'll have to start over with a new package of yeast.

While you're waiting for your yeast to prove itself you might as well assemble the dry ingredients in a medium-size bowl. Once you're sure your yeast is good, add the oil and the yeast mixture to the flour and salt and stir, or mix with your hands if you're the adventurous sort. You won't get very far before the dough balls up and doesn't want to absorb any more flour; don't worry, that's normal. Sprinkle a little flour on your nice, clean countertop and dump out the whole mixture onto it. It's time to knead.

Kneading dough is a bit more art than science, and there's no real "right" way to do it, as long as you get it thoroughly mixed and stretched. Don't work too hard at it; you're going to be kneading it for 10 minutes or so and you don't want to wear yourself out at the start.

Your dough should be a little sticky; before you start, pat your hands with flour to keep them from sticking. If the dough is really, really sticky, work some more flour into it as you knead. Soon enough the dough should become less sticky and easier to work, in a kind of magical way; now's the time to really start working it, stretching it out and squishing it with your hands. Don't be afraid to treat it rough; it likes it. The more you work it the stretchier and more elastic it will be, which is what you want for pizza dough.

After about 10 minutes the dough should be nice and stretchy, still moist and tacky but not sticky or gooey. If it seems really tough and dry you've probably added too much flour. Don't worry; it happens. You can still use it; maybe knead it a little longer and remember to try not to add as much flour next time. Pizza dough's not hard, but it takes a little practice to get it perfect.

Form the dough into a tight little ball. You'll need a clean bowl that's at least twice the size of your dough ball for the dough to rise in. Put a little oil (about 2 teaspoons, but it doesn't have to be that precise) in the bowl, and put your dough ball in it and swirl it around a little, then flip it over. The idea here is to get both the bowl and your ball of dough covered with a thin film of oil. Cover the bowl with a clean, damp towel or plastic wrap and set it in a warm place. Go away for about an hour.

When you come back your dough ball should've doubled in size, more or less. Here's the fun part: uncover your dough and give it a firm, solid punch so it deflates. Sprinkle some more flour onto your countertop and dump the dough out onto it and start kneading. It should be stretchier and more pliable than it was before. Knead it for only about a minute, or until it's less like a sponge and more like dough again. Put it back in the bowl and cover it so it can rest.

How long? It's up to you. You can freeze the dough now if you want and then defrost it and continue later. If you're impatient you can wait as little as ten minutes, but your dough won't be very stretchy. An hour or two would be good. Either way, when you've waited long enough (and when your oven is hot enough; preheat to 500°F or as hot as you dare), sprinkle your countertop with flour (again), take your dough ball out of the bowl, and cut it in two. Put one portion of dough back into the bowl.

Now it's time to stretch. Like kneading, stretching is an art and you'll get better with practice, so don't be discouraged if your first couple of pizzas are uneven or small. Don't expect to be throwing it up in the air and catching it like they do in the pizzeria; those guys are seasoned pros. Again, there's no right way; whatever works is good, but here's what I do: with my hands I flatten out the dough a little, and then I roll it out with a rolling pin until it's about a foot in diameter. Then I pick it up on one side and let gravity help me stretch it out; I work my way around it, trying to stretch it into an even circle, until I start to worry that it will tear. Then I sprinkle my pizza tray with a little cornmeal and set down the crust on it, pat it out a little bit more, and then apply the toppings. If the dough is just right and your stretching technique works, you should be able to get two 14-inch thin-crust pizzas from this recipe; but like I said, it takes practice, so if your pizzas are parallelogram-shaped or lumpy, just say they're "rustic" and don't sweat it.

Now we're ready to make some pizzas!

Pizza Sauce

Pizza sauce is a simple thing, a little tomato sauce, a little garlic, a few herbs. It doesn't take much to create Brooklyn's most beloved sauce. The mistake some home cooks make is overseasoning it with all kinds of Italian spice mixes and whatnot—all it really needs is a subtle hint of the herbs.

2 teaspoons olive oil

2 cloves garlic, minced

1 teaspoon dried oregano

½ teaspoon dried thyme

1 teaspoon salt

A few dashes fresh black pepper

1 (22-ounce) can tomatoes in juice (plum tomatoes if you can find them)

2 tablespoons tomato paste

In a saucepan over medium-low heat sauté the garlic in the olive oil for about 2 minutes, being careful not to burn the garlic. Add the herbs, salt, and pepper. Stir in the tomatoes, crushing them in your hand as you add them. Add about half the juice from the canned tomatoes, and the tomato paste. Increase the heat a bit and cook for about 10 minutes, stirring and crushing the tomatoes as you go. If the sauce looks too chunky, you can puree half of it in a blender (see Punk Points) and add it back to the rest of the sauce. Let cool to room temperature before using on pizzas. You can store whatever you don't use in the fridge for 3 or 4 days, or you can freeze it for up to 3 months.

PUNK POINTS

If you are using a blender to puree the sauce, let the sauce cool a bit so that the steam doesn't cause the blender lid to pop off and hot sauce to splatter everywhere. Once the sauce has cooled, give it a few pulses in the blender, lift the lid to let steam escape, and repeat.

PIZZAS AND PASTAS

VEGAN WITH A VENGEANCE

Maybe you've noticed that my name sorta rhymes with pizza? I know someone else who realized that—everyone I've ever met EVER—from my kindergarten class on up. Well, it's finally come in handy! I can name a pizza after myself. Of course this pizza is awesome or it wouldn't be my namesake: salty olives, fragrant pesto, creamy tofu ricotta, and yummy cremini mushrooms.

> **Pizza dough for 2 pizzas (page 128)**
> **Pizza Sauce (previous recipe)**
> **Basil-Tofu Ricotta (recipe follows)**
> **Classic Pesto (recipe follows)**
> **⅓ cup pitted and halved kalamata olives**
> **⅓ cup thinly sliced cremini mushrooms**
> **Cornmeal for the pan**
> **Olive oil for drizzling and brushing**

Preheat oven to 500° F .

Roll your dough out as described on page 129. Use the back of a big spoon to spread the pizza sauce onto the dough—use about ⅓ cup or so—leaving about 1½ inch of space bare around the circumference. You should still be able to see some of the crust underneath—if you add too much it may make your dough soggy. Spoon the ricotta on, in mounds about 2 tablespoonfuls apiece—you'll want five mounds of it or so. Do the same with the pesto. You should have circles of pesto and ricotta but still be able to see the red sauce underneath.

Scatter half the olives and mushrooms on top of the pizza. Drizzle a little olive oil on the mushrooms so that they don't dry out while cooking. Use a pastry brush to brush the crust around the circumference with a thin layer of olive oil.

Place the pizza in the bottom of the oven on a pizza stone. Check it after 8 minutes. Once the crust is lightly browned your pizza is ready. It can take up to 12 minutes. Remove from oven and transfer to a large cutting board to slice. Proceed to your next pizza; by this point you should be feeling like a real pizza guy.

VEGAN WITH A VENGEANCE

Classic Pesto

"When in doubt—pesto" is my mantra. I serve it whenever I'm feeling lazy and want to cook something delicious that everyone will love. The nutritional yeast makes it creamier but it is entirely optional.

> ½ cup walnuts
> 3 cups packed basil leaves
> 3 cloves garlic, smashed and coarsely chopped
> 1½ teaspoons coarse salt
> ½ cup extra-virgin olive oil, or more to taste
> ¼ cup nutritional yeast (optional)
> 2 teaspoons lemon juice

Toast the walnuts in a toaster oven at 350°F for 5 minutes or on a baking sheet in a conventional oven for 10 minutes, turning once.

Combine the walnuts, basil, garlic, and salt in a food processor or blender and process while you add the olive oil in a slow, steady stream. Add the nutritional yeast and lemon juice, and pulse to combine. The sauce should be the consistency of a slightly grainy paste, not a puree.

VEGAN WITH A VENGEANCE

Basil-Tofu Ricotta

Use as a filling for stuffed shells, mixed with tomato sauce in pasta, or as a topping for pizza.

> **1 pound firm tofu, pressed**
> **2 teaspoon lemon juice**
> **1 clove garlic, minced**
> **¼ teaspoon salt**
> **Dash fresh black pepper**
> **Handful fresh basil leaves, finely chopped (ten leaves or so)**
> **2 teaspoons olive oil**
> **¼ cup nutritional yeast**

In a large bowl, mush the tofu up with your hands, till it's crumbly.

Add the lemon juice, garlic, salt, pepper, and basil. Mush with your hands again; this time you want it to get very mushy so squeeze through your fingers and mush until it reaches the consistency of ricotta cheese. This may take 2 to 5 minutes.

Add the olive oil, stir with a fork. Add the nutritional yeast and mix all ingredients well. Use a fork now, because the oil will make it sticky. Cover and refrigerate until ready to use.

VEGAN WITH
VENGEANCE

Potato and Tempeh Sausage Pizza

Potatoes on pizza? How zany. This was a popular topping choice on The Post Punk Kitchen message boards and I have to say, the boards are never wrong. Try to cut the potatoes as evenly as possible so that when they cook they are crispy outside and chewy inside. The fennel and tempeh are a match made in heaven, and the chewy potatoes make the marriage work. I love this pizza as is, but if you would like to add soy cheese I can't stop you.

> Pizza Sauce (page 130)
> 1 cup shredded mozzarella soy cheese (optional)
> Tempeh Crumbles (page 22)
> 1 medium-size russet potato, scrubbed, cut in half and thinly sliced (slices
>   should be under ¼ inch thick)
> 1 medium-size fennel bulb, trimmed, very thinly sliced
> 4 cloves garlic, thinly sliced
> Olive oil for drizzling and brushing

Preheat oven to 500° F.

Roll out your dough as described on page 129. Use the back of a big spoon to spread the pizza sauce onto the dough—use about ⅓ cup or so—leaving about 1½ inches of empty space around the circumference of the dough. You should still be able to see some of the crust underneath—if you add too much sauce, it may make your dough soggy.

Sprinkle on the cheese, if using. Scatter half the other toppings randomly over the sauce, making sure that the potatoe slices and fennel lay flat for even cooking. Drizzle a little olive oil on the garlic, potatoes, and fennel so that they don't dry out while cooking. Use a pastry brush to brush the edge of the crust with a thin layer of olive oil.

Place the crust in the bottom of the oven on a pizza stone. Check it after 8 minutes. Once the crust is lightly browned, your pizza is ready. It can take up to 12 minutes. Remove from oven and transfer to a large cutting board to slice. Proceed to your next pizza; by this point you should feel like you're fresh off the boat from the Old Country.

Some Pizza Tips from a Brooklyn Girl Who Knows from Pizza

✗ Don't overload your pizza with toppings, (a) because veggies contain water that will cook out as it heats, and this water can seep into your pizza dough and we don't want that; and (b) because the sauce and dough is delicious; it's nice to have an olive here and there, but if there's olives or mushrooms or what-have-you all over the thing it takes away from the pizza experience.

✗ Once your pizza dough is prepared keep it wrapped in plastic wrap—it dries out fast! If it does dry out in some spots just do your best to rip off the dry parts and use the rest of it.

✗ You need a pizza stone for awesome crust. Sure, without one you may be able to get a serviceable crust—but for awesome crust a stone is a must. Its intense concentrated heat will ensure that you don't wind up with a soggy crust. If for some reason you refuse to procure a stone, place the pizza tray directly on the bottom of the oven in the last 2 to 3 minutes of cooking. If a pizza stone is too pricy you can use a "quarry tile" available at gardening supply stores; they only cost a few dollars. That tip is often attributed to Alton Brown but I remember reading it in a Julia Child book way before Alton Brown shot to fame.

✗ Experiment with textures and flavors. As long as you're not putting worn socks on the pizza it will probably taste good. I'm giving you a few of my favorite pizzas here but also try these toppings

Roasted Red Peppers
Roasted Brussels Sprouts (page 125)
Pineapple and Tempeh Bacon
Artichoke Hearts
Roasted Garlic (page 67)

VEGAN WITH A VENGEANCE

Green Goddess Garlic Pizza

This is a delicious and beautiful pizza that is various shades of green and has a delicious roasted garlic base plus more garlic on top for good measure. Because all goddesses should have garlic breath. This has a lot of components that are labor intensive but you will have the makings for dinner for the next two nights-use the remaining Garden Puree and pesto in pasta.

2 Pizza Crusts (page 128)
1 bunch spinach, well rinsed, leaves only
Salt
2 bulbs roasted garlic (page 67)
1 tablespoon olive oil plus extra for drizzling and brushing
Classic Pesto (page 132)
Garden Puree (recipe follows)
1 cup chopped broccoli florets
½ cup pitted green olives
4 cloves garlic, thinly sliced
Cornmeal

Preheat oven to 500°F

Roll your dough out as described on page 129. Cover with plastic wrap or a kitchen towel until ready to use.

Fill a skillet with about an inch of water and bring to a boil. Add the spinach and sprinkle with salt; cook until spinach is wilted, about a minute. Drain in a colander and run some cold water over it; when cool enough to handle, press out as much water as you can. Set aside.

Remove the roasted garlic cloves from their skins (you should be able to just squeeze them and the garlic will come out). Place in a bowl and mash with a strong fork. Add a tablespoon of the olive oil and mash into a paste.

Spread half the garlic paste on the pizza dough. Spoon dollops of pesto on top, about 2 inches apart. Mound here and there 2 tablespoons worth per mound of Garden Puree. Place half the wilted spinach, olives, broccoli florets, and sliced garlic randomly upon the pizza. Drizzle the vegetable toppings with a little olive oil to prevent their drying out. Brush the edge of the crust with olive oil.

Place the crust in the bottom of the oven on a pizza stone. Check it after 8 minutes. Once the crust is lightly browned, your pizza is ready. It can take up to 12 minutes. Remove from oven and transfer to a large cutting board to slice. Proceed to your next pizza; by this point you should feel like you're serving pizza in a vegan villa in Italy.

Green Garden Puree

This is a fresh-tasting thick ricotta-like puree that is delicious as a lasagne or ravioli filling, or as a pasta or pizza topping.

1 pound asparagus, ends discarded, chopped into 3-inch lengths
1 pound green beans, halved, ends removed and discarded
1 cup frozen peas
1 cup slivered almonds
2 cloves garlic
1 cup loosely packed flat-leaf parsley
4 scallions, green parts only, coarsely chopped
2 tablespoons extra-virgin olive oil
Juice of ½ lemon
⅛ teaspoon ground or grated fresh nutmeg
1 pound extra-firm tofu
1 cup chopped basil leaves

Have ready a large bowl of ice water.

Bring a large pot of salted water to boil. Add the asparagus and green beans; boil for 2 minutes. Add the frozen peas and boil for 2 more minutes. Drain vegetables and submerge in the ice water to stop cooking.

Pulse the almonds into a fine powder. Add the boiled vegetables, garlic, parsley, scallions, olive oil, lemon juice, and nutmeg; puree until smooth.

In a large bowl, mash the tofu with your hands until it has a ricotta-like consistency. Add the puree and mix well. Fold in the basil. Cover and refrigerate until ready to use.

VEGAN WITH A VENGEANCE

There is no substitute, well, I should say, no good substitute for homemade pastas. Gnocchi are a nice place to start in your pasta-making journey because they are easy, delicious, and pretty difficult to mess up. If you are unfamiliar with gnocchi, they are a small, cute potato dumpling. There are a lot of accoutrements you can spend money on to give your gnocchi the perfect ridges that you find in the store-bought or restaurant variety but I find that a long fork works just fine. This is my basic recipe to get you started but I've listed some of my favorite variations below. Make sure to try those as well! Serve with Classic Pesto (page 132), Sun-dried Tomato Pesto (page 183), or a simple tomato sauce.

> **2 pounds russet potatoes, washed and scrubbed**
> **½ teaspoon salt**
> **2 tablespoons olive oil**
> **1½ to ¾ cups all-purpose flour**

Preheat oven to 400°F.

Poke four or five holes all over the potatoes. Bake them (you don't need a tray or foil, right on the oven rack is fine) for 45 minutes to an hour, depending on the size. Do a test after 45 minutes; they should be very tender. Use tongs to remove them; place on a cooling rack and let them cool completely. This could take half an hour.

Remove the skins from the cooled potatoes and place them in a large mixing bowl. Add the olive oil and salt and mash very well. You don't want to puree them, that will make the gnocchi sticky, just mash them until they have very few lumps. Add the flour in handfuls and incorporate it into the potatoes. Once you've added half the flour you can turn the dough onto a floured countertop to work it there. Keep adding flour and lightly kneading the dough until a smooth, unsticky but not dry dough is formed.

Divide the dough into thirds and roll each portion into a rope that is about ½ inch thick. Use a pizza wheel or a knife to cut the ropes into ¾-inch-long pieces. Now comes the fun part (well, I think it's fun)—flour your hands and use your thumb to roll each piece of gnocchi gently down the tines of a fork. Each piece should be able to do about half a roll before reaching the end of the fork so the final result should be that one side of the gnocchi has an indent from your thumb and one side has ridges from the fork.

At this point you can sprinkle with flour and freeze any gnocchi you aren't using. To cook them immediately bring a large pot of water to a boil. Salt the water liberally and cook the gnocchi in three batches. Within 2 minutes they should rise to the surface; let them cook just under a minute longer and remove them with a slotted

VEGAN WITH A VENGEANCE

spoon. Transfer them to a large plate so that they aren't putting weight on each other and sauce them as soon as you can. I like them with either a simple tomato sauce or sautéed briefly with pesto and veggies.

VARIATIONS:

Herbed Gnocchi: After mashing the potatoes, add 2 tablespoons of chopped fresh herbs, such as oregano, thyme, and rosemary.

Sun-dried Tomato Gnocchi: Use only 1½ pounds of potatoes. Soak 1 cup of chopped sun-dried tomatoes in hot water. Cover and let sit until soft (10 to 15 minutes). Reserve ¼ cup of the soaking water and drain away the rest. Puree the tomatoes in a blender or food processor until smooth, adding the soaking water by the tablespoon if needed to achieve a smooth puree. Add the tomatoes to the mashed potatoes. You may need to add ¼ cup or so more flour to the mixture.

Spinach Gnocchi: Chop finely one bunch of well-rinsed spinach. Cook in a skillet over medium heat in about ¼ cup of water until it is completely wilted. Place in a strainer and press all the water out. Add to the potatoes after they have been mashed.

PUNK POINTS

The best way to freeze gnocchi and not have them stick together is to line up the uncooked gnocchi on a cutting board or baking sheet (or anything big and flat) lined with parchment paper and sprinkled lightly with flour. Place the pan in the freezer for about an hour. Then you can transfer the gnocchi to zip-top bags or lidded plastic containers and place back in the freezer for up to 3 months. When ready to cook, follow the directions in this recipe.

VEGAN WITH A VENGEANCE

Orecchiette with Cherry Tomatoes and Kalamata Tapenade

Salty olives and tart, sweet cherry tomatoes taste luscious in this easy-to-prepare dish. I like to use orecchiette here because they cup the thick sauce nicely—but of course you can use whatever pasta you want to. This recipe is for a ½ pound of pasta, which is supposedly four servings. If you are like most people I know, four servings = two servings, so plan accordingly. The tapenade recipe makes enough for a pound of pasta, though, so you can double the pasta and still have plenty of tapenade-y goodness to go around. If you have some left over, I suggest spreading it on toasted French bread for crostini or adding it to your sammiches throughout the week.

> ½ **pound orecchiette**
> 1 **tablespoon olive oil**
> 1 **medium-size red onion, sliced into thin half moons (about 1 cup)**
> 1 **pound cherry tomatoes, halved**

> FOR THE TAPENADE:
> 1½ **cups kalamata olives, pitted**
> 3 **tablespoons capers, drained**
> 2 **cloves garlic, chopped**
> **Handful fresh parsley (about ½ cup lightly packed)**
> ½ **teaspoon dried oregano**
> ½ **teaspoon dried tarragon**
> **A few dashes fresh ground pepper**
> 1 **tablespoon red wine vinegar**
> 2 **tablespoons olive oil**

Prepare the tapenade:
   Combine all the tapenade ingredients in a blender or food processor.

Prepare everything else:
   Prepare the pasta according to its package directions. While the pasta is boiling, sauté the onions and cherry tomatoes in the olive oil over medium heat for about 7 minutes.

140 | PIZZAS AND PASTAS

Reserve a ½ cup of cooking water from the pasta and drain the rest. Add the pasta to the tomatoes and sauté for a few seconds (I use a pasta spoon to sauté because it mixes everything well and doesn't crush anything). Add 1 cup of the tapenade and the reserved pasta water; stir to coat. When the tapenade is heated through it is ready to serve.

VEGAN WITH A VENGEANCE

Fettuccine Alfreda

This recipe is from my old friends the Baltimorons, but by the time this recipe was invented they had moved to Minneapolis. Anyway, one of them found a bag of pine nuts and they taught me to make this sauce, or something like it. I can't exactly duplicate the recipe because I think a lot of the flavor came from the fact that the pine nuts were "found." It's yummy to add some sautéed veggies on top of the pasta and some Grilled Tofu (page 145) wouldn't hurt either. Serve it with some home brew that may not have come out quite right. I guess it's like a vegan fettuccine Alfredo, but so so so much better.

½ pound fettuccine
2 teaspoons olive oil
1 medium-size onion, chopped into big chunks
4 cloves garlic, chopped
½ cup water or vegetable broth
2 teaspoons yellow mustard
½ cup pine nuts, toasted (see Punk Points)
2 teaspoons soy sauce or Bragg Liquid Aminos
2 teaspoons chile powder
1 cup nutritional yeast
½ teaspoon salt
A few dashes fresh black pepper

Prepare pasta according to package directions.

In a skillet over moderate heat, sauté the onions in olive oil for 3 minutes, until just slightly softened. Add the garlic, sauté for 2 more minutes. Transfer to a blender, add all the other ingredients, and blend away. It should be somewhat smooth but still a bit grainy.

This amount should be enough for four servings of pasta. You can reheat it in a saucepan over low heat if you need to. If you want to make it thicker, add more nutritional yeast by the tablespoon. To thin it out, add pasta water by the tablespoon.

Drain the pasta and transfer it to a plate, spoon the sauce over the top, add veggies and tofu if using, and serve.

PUNK POiNTS

To toast pine nuts, heat a heavy-bottomed skillet over medium-high heat. Toss in the pine nuts and stir frequently for about 5 minutes, until they are lightly browned.

VEGAN WITH A VENGEANCE

I can never answer the question "What is your favorite kind of food?" because, well, "favorite" questions are sort of arbitrary and there are just too many answers to choose from. Yet people always seem to ask. My standard answer is "Brooklyn food," because it seems like there isn't one culinary palate that dominates my beloved borough. So here you will find a diverse selection of dishes inspired by every corner of the world and I never had to leave Brooklyn for inspiration.

ENTRÉES

Tofu is a delicious protein that can be quite versatile once you get the hang of using it. If you've been unsuccessful using it in the past, try these tips and I guarantee you will be a tofu pro in no time (well, in about the hour it takes to press it).

The most important thing to know when dealing with tofu is that for a nice firm texture you will need to press all the water out. This will allow any marinade you soak it in to penetrate as much as possible, and will help it to crisp up when frying.

Start with a drained block of extra firm tofu and place it between a clean kitchen towel or 3 or 4 paper towels on each side. Place a heavy, level object (like a hardcover book) over the tofu. For good measure you can place another heavy object on top of the book. I often use a few cans of beans or sometimes a castiron pan. Let it sit like that for half an hour, then flip it over for another half an hour.

If you don't have a full hour to press the tofu, you can "quick press" it. Cut it into 4 even slices widthwise and press each slice very gently between your hands to get the water out. Then wrap each slice in paper towels and place under a heavy object as described above for as long as you can (at least 10 minutes).

Freezing tofu creates a different, chewier texture. Freeze it in its packaging and let it thaw completely before pressing it. It's very important that the tofu thaws completely or else it will have a spongy unappealing texture. Frozen tofu tastes great crumbled into chilis and stews.

Don't limit your tofu cuts to dices and thin rectangles. Below are some of my favorite ways to slice tofu. I find that different shapes and sizes can really up the visual aspects of any dish.

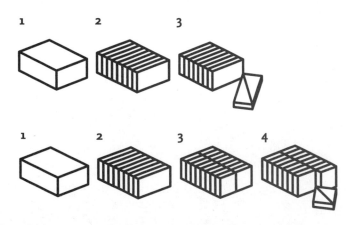

VEGAN WITH A VENGEANCE

Marinated Tofu

I eat some version of the following recipes for dinner a few times a week because they are so easy yet produce amazing results. It's hard to remember that simple things can be extraordinary but these recipes prove just that. I've listed the marinade ingredients but the cooking methods are the same for both.

italian Tofu

SERVES 4 (OR 2, IF YOU'RE VERY HUNGRY)

1 pound extra-firm tofu, drained and pressed
½ cup white cooking wine
2 tablespoon olive oil
2 tablespoons balsamic vinegar
2 tablespoons Bragg Liquid Aminos or tamari
2 tablespoons fresh lemon juice
2 cloves garlic, smashed
A big pinch each dried basil, marjoram, and thyme

Asian Tofu

SERVES 4 (OR 2 IF YOU'RE REALLY HUNGRY)

This tofu goes great with Wasabi Mashed Potatoes (page 110) and asparagus.

1 pound extra-firm tofu, drained and pressed
½ cup mirin
3 tablespoons tamari
2 tablespoons rice wine vinegar
1 tablespoon sesame oil
2 teaspoons Asian chile sauce
A 1-inch chunk ginger, peeled and coarsely chopped
2 cloves garlic, smashed

Prepare the marinade:
    Combine all marinade ingredients in a wide shallow bowl.

VEGAN WITH
VENGEANCE

For grilled tofu:

Cut the tofu widthwise into four equal pieces. Marinate for an hour, flipping over after 30 minutes.

Grease a stovetop grill pan (preferably cast iron) with vegetable oil. Preheat over a high flame for about 3 minutes. Use tongs to distribute the tofu slabs evenly onto the grill. Gently use the tongs to press the tofu into the grill ridges, to get nice dark lines. Cook for 3 minutes on one side without lifting, then turn the slabs 90 degrees to create a crosshatched pattern on the bottom of the tofu. Cook for 2 minutes, then flip over and cook for another 2 minutes. Move to a cutting board and cut each piece diagonally across into two triangles with a sharp knife. (See illustration in "Taming Your Tofu.")

For baked tofu:

Preheat oven to 400°F.

Cut the tofu widthwise into eight equal pieces. Marinate for an hour, flipping after 30 minutes.

Place the tofu on a baking sheet and bake for 20 minutes. Flip over and bake another 10 minutes. Place in the broiler for about 3 more minutes for extra chewiness.

PUNK POINTS

Don't throw the tofu out with the bathwater; reserve your marinade and get creative. Remove the garlic and/or ginger and mix in a little water and arrowroot or cornstarch, then heat it up and you've got yourself a gravy. Or, use it to stir-fry broccoli or asparagus for a nice, fast side dish: heat up some vegetable oil over high heat, then add your chopped vegetables, pouring on splashes of the marinade as you cook.

VEGAN WITH A VENGEANCE

Stewed Tofu and Potatoes in Miso Gravy

Even though this recipe calls for miso, it has a very American "meat and potatoes" taste and texture. The potatoes are perfectly creamy yet still firm and the tofu is deliciously plump and packed with flavor. It's a great meal to reheat the next day. I use chickpea miso, available at supermarkets, for this savory dish but you can use whichever kind you like.

> 2 tablespoons arrowroot or cornstarch
> 1 cup vegetable broth
> 2 cups thinly sliced cremini mushrooms
> 4 tablespoons olive oil
> 1 large onion, quartered and thinly sliced (about 2 cups)
> 2 shallots, minced (about 1/3 cup)
> 4 cloves garlic, coarsely chopped
> 1 teaspoon fresh thyme, chopped
> Several dashes fresh black pepper
> 1 1/2 cups white wine
> 1 tablespoon tamari or soy sauce
> 3 tablespoons chickpea miso
> 1 pound small Yukon gold or fingerling potatoes, halved
>   (or a larger potato cut into 1 1/4-inch chunks)
> 1 pound tofu, pressed, cut into eighths widthwise, and then
>   cut into two long isosceles triangles (see page 144)

Mix the arrowroot with the vegetable broth to dissolve, and set aside.

In a large skillet sauté the mushrooms in 2 tablespoons of the olive oil over medium high heat for 5 to 7 minutes, until browned and most of the water has evaporated. Remove from pan and set aside.

Sauté onions and shallots in the remaining 2 tablespoons of olive oil for 5 to 7 minutes until slightly browned; add the garlic, thyme, and black pepper, sauté for 2 more minutes. Stir in the white wine, arrowroot mixture, tamari, and miso. Bring to a boil, then lower heat to a simmer; the miso should be completely dissolved. Add the mushrooms, potatoes, and tofu. The pan will be crowded but make sure that all

VEGAN WITH A VENGEANCE

Fizzle says:

Miso is prized for its many nutritional bene-fits, among them fighting radiation sickness as evidenced after the Chernobyl nuclear accidents—miso was used to prevent radiation disorders. Let's hope you aren't eating it for that reason, rather for its richness in trace minerals and dietary fiber.

potatoes are mostly sub-merged in the gravy, it's okay if they stick out a little. Cover and simmer over low heat for 25 to 30 minutes, until the potatoes are very tender.

Serve over mashed sweet potatoes or mashed potatoes or as a stew with some good crusty bread.

VEGAN WITH A VENGEANCE

BBQ Pomegranate Tofu

I love the floral taste of pomegranate and a little of the molasses goes a long way. I realize pomegranate molasses is an esoteric ingredient, but it's one of those things I was dying to try and it was well worth hunting out. I was even able to find it at the shabby grocery store around the corner from my apartment, but I think any well-stocked gourmet store will have it; if not try a Middle Eastern grocery. You can double the tofu and still have enough sauce for the dish. I like to steam some veggies to go along with it and smother them in the extra sauce; served with the Coconut Rice (page 109) you've created something sublime.

FOR THE TOFU:
  1 pound tofu, drained and pressed, sliced into eighths
  2 tablespoons peanut oil
  1 tablespoon tamari

FOR THE BBQ SAUCE:
  1 tablespoon peanut oil
  1 cup shallots, minced
  2 cloves garlic, minced
  ½ teaspoon Chinese five-spice powder
  2 cups vegetable broth
  A couple dashes fresh black pepper
  1 (6-ounce) can tomato paste
  2 tablespoons creamy all-natural peanut butter
  2 tablespoons pomegranate molasses
  2 tablespoons tamari or soy sauce
  ¼ cup pure maple syrup
  1 teaspoon hot sauce (or more to taste)
  1 teaspoon liquid smoke

FOR GARNISH:
  ½ cup pomegranate seeds

Preheat oven to 350°F. In a 9 × 13-inch (preferably glass or ceramic) baking pan, turn the tofu in the peanut oil and tamari to coat on both sides. Bake for 15 minutes, then flip the slices and bake for 15 minutes more. Meanwhile, prepare the sauce.

In a saucepan over medium heat, sauté the shallots in the peanut oil for about 5 minutes, add the garlic and five-spice powder, and sauté 1 minute more. Add the

VEGAN WITH A VENGEANCE

broth and bring to a simmer. Add the rest of the ingredients (except for the pomegranate seeds) and bring to a boil. Lower heat and simmer for 15 to 20 minutes, stirring frequently.

At this point, your tofu should be done baking. Smother the tofu with the BBQ sauce, return to oven, and bake 15 minutes more. Remove from oven. Serve with Coconut Rice and garnish with the pomegranate seeds.

Fizzle says:

Pomegranates are delicious but a bit of a pain to eat. The only edible part of the grapefruit-size fruit is the outer casing of the seeds, which means you have to split open the fruit, take out the seeds, and remove the pits from the seeds to enjoy the sweet, tangy juice. They're very yummy, though, and if convenience is your thing you can buy pomegranate juice, pomegranate sauce, grenadine (made from pomegranates), and other stuff.

VEGAN WITH A VENGEANCE

Horseradish- and Coriander-Crusted Tofu

Most people are familiar with horseradish of the jarred variety, and that's all fair and well, but it's a whole other thing to experience this spicy root freshly grated. Briefly cooking the horseradish cuts down on the heat quite a bit, so don't worry that it will be too spicy for you. I serve this with a simple tartar sauce (2 parts Vegannaise, 1 part sweet pickle relish) and Wasabi Mashed Potatoes (page 110).

FOR THE MARINADE:

½ cup white cooking wine

1 tablespoon tamari or soy sauce

Juice of 1 lemon

2 cloves garlic, smashed

1 pound extra-firm tofu, drained and pressed for at least an hour, sliced length-wise into eighths

FOR THE CRUST:

⅓ cup panko (Japanese bread crumbs; if you can't find these, use unflavored, preferably whole wheat bread crumbs)

⅓ cup very loosely packed chopped fresh mint

3 tablespoons fresh horseradish, grated

Finely grated zest of 1 lemon

1 tablespoon coriander seeds, crushed (see page 21)

⅛ teaspoon salt

A few dashes fresh ground black pepper

1 tablespoon oil

Prepare the marinade:

Mix all ingredients together in a shallow bowl; marinate the tofu for at least 1 hour, turning occasionally.

Prepare the dish:

Preheat oven to 400°F. Line a baking pan with foil and lightly coat in oil or spray with nonstick cooking spray.

In a shallow bowl, mix together the bread crumbs, mint, horseradish, lemon zest, coriander, salt, and black pepper. Sprinkle with the olive oil and combine with a fork.

Press each piece of tofu firmly into the mixture on both sides, one piece at a time. Take a small amount of the panko mixture and press it into the top side of the tofu (the underside will be less crusty because less crumbs stick to it; just a little sprinkle of crumbs should suffice on that side, otherwise too many will burn). Place each slice in the prepared pan.

Bake for 15 minutes. Transfer to broiler for another 5 minutes. Serve.

Fizzle says:

Once the horseradish is grated be prepared to use it immediately; it will develop a bitter taste if left around for too long.

VEGAN WITH A VENGEANCE

Mango-Ginger Tofu

The summer that I invented this mango tofu little could stop me from bringing it to any function that would have me. We had it grilled on the Fourth of July on a rooftop in Brooklyn while watching fireworks over the East River. The next week I brought it to a Leonard Cohen tribute concert. And then we enjoyed it again on my Mom's birthday. I started to get self-conscious that people might think it was the only thing I knew how to make, and they'd start calling me "Isa with the mango tofu," but really it's that good, you won't be able to stop yourself. Choose mangoes that are ripe but not overripe; they should give only slightly if you squeeze them.

FOR THE MARINADE:
2 teaspoons peanut oil
3 cloves garlic
¼ cup fresh ginger, coarsely chopped
1 jalapeño, seeded and chopped
2 large mangoes, peeled and coarsely chopped (see Punk Points, page 154)
¼ cup pure maple syrup
1 cup white cooking wine or vegetable broth
2 tablespoon rice vinegar (use apple cider vinegar or red wine vinegar if you don't have rice)
Juice of 2 limes
1 cup orange juice
¼ teaspoon ground allspice
Fresh black pepper to taste
Dash of salt

FOR THE TOFU:
2 pounds extra-firm tofu, drained and pressed cut into isosceles shapes (page 144)
1 mango, sliced into long, thin slices
1 red bell pepper, seeded and cut in long, thin slices

Make the marinade:

Preheat a medium-size saucepan over moderate heat; combine the oil, garlic, ginger, and jalapeño, and sauté for 7 minutes, being careful not to burn the garlic. Add the chopped mango and sauté for 5 more minutes.

Add the maple syrup and wine, cover and simmer for 35 minutes. Uncover and simmer for 5 more minutes.

153

ENTREES

VEGAN WITH A VENGEANCE

Add the vinegar, lime juice, orange juice, allspice, black pepper, and salt; let cool, then transfer the mixture to blender and puree until smooth.

Place the prepared tofu in the marinade in a sealable plastic bag or a tightly lidded plastic container. Marinate in the fridge for at least an hour and up to overnight.

Bake the tofu:

Preheat oven to 375°F.

Reserve about half of the marinade. Lay the marinated tofu in a single layer in a large rimmed baking sheet or baking pan. Bake for 20 minutes. Flip over the tofu and add more marinade. Coat the peppers and remaining mango in the reserved marinade and add them to the pan. Bake another 15 minutes.

Heat the remaining marinade in a saucepan and put in a bowl on the table (or floor, whereever you're eating) so guests can pour it over the tofu. Serve over jasmine rice with a steamed vegetable, such as asparagus or broccoli.

PUNK POINTS

There are several fancy ways to chop a mango but the way I usually do it is the most reliable (and of course the messiest). First, I peel it with a serrated peeler to prevent slipping. Then I place it on a cutting board, slice against the flat part of the pit, and then repeat on the other sides. Then simply chop the fruit slices as needed.

VEGAN WITH A VENGEANCE

Pumpkin Seed–Crusted Tofu with Baked Pumpkin and Cranberry Relish

Every year we buy a couple of pumpkins to cook with the best of intentions but they end up as decoration until they meet their demise. Well, not this year! This recipe utilizes the whole pumpkin—the pulp and the seeds. It's fun to pull together and it's got that homespun feel since you toast the seeds yourself. It's also really crunchy and flavorful, especially topped off with the cranberry relish. I hope this becomes an autumn tradition for you as it has for me.

> 3 to 3½ pound sugar pumpkin
> 8 teaspoons canola oil plus extra for deep-frying
> ½ cup cornstarch
> ¼ cup fresh oregano, chopped
> ¼ teaspoon salt
> 1 pound extra-firm tofu, drained and pressed, sliced lengthwise into eighths
> 1 cup all-purpose flour
> 1 cup water

Preheat oven to 300°F.

Carve out the top of the pumpkin with a paring knife and slice the pumpkin in half with a chef's knife. Remove the seeds and clean them in a strainer under running water (the holes should be big enough for the stringy bits to escape). Set the pumpkin aside to prepare as described below. Dry the seeds thoroughly by laying on a paper towel or kitchen towel; pat the tops with another towel to remove any moisture. Measure ¾ cup of seeds and transfer them to a rimmed baking sheet. Sprinkle with 2 teaspoons of oil, toss to coat. Bake for 20 minutes, flipping occasionally. They should be toasted a golden brown to a deep golden brown. Transfer to a bowl to cool. Meanwhile, prepare the pumpkin.

Adjust the oven temperature to 350°F. Cut the pumpkin into slices that are about 2 inches wide at the widest point. Lightly oil the slices with canola oil. Place on a rimmed baking sheet and bake for about 45 minutes, until tender and lightly browned.

When the seeds have cooled, transfer them to a food processor and pulse until crumbly; the texture should range from ground to coarse and chunky. In a shallow bowl mix the seeds with the cornstarch, oregano, and salt. Place the flour in another bowl, the water in another, and line up your three bowls: flour, water, and the seed mixture.

VEGAN WITH VENGEANCE

Heat ¼ inch of oil over moderate heat in a heavy-bottomed skillet, preferably cast iron. The heat should be between 320 and 350°F; if you don't have a thermometer test the oil by dropping a pinch of the seed mixture in; if bubbles form rapidly around the seeds, the oil is ready.

Dip the tofu on both sides into the flour, then into the water, then into the seed mixture on both sides until the tofu is well coated with seeds. Repeat until all eight pieces are ready. Using tongs, lower the pieces into the oil (you may have to do it in two batches). Fry for 3 minutes on one side and about 2½ minutes on the second side. Remove from the oil and transfer to flattened paper bags or paper towels to drain the excess oil. Serve with roasted pumpkin.

PUNK POINTS

When frying, the temperature of the oil is really important. Too hot and the food will burn; too cool and it won't cook properly. A frying thermometer is a pretty important accessory to have for this kinda stuff. If you don't have one, there are several methods to test if the oil is ready. One is to drop in some crumbs and see if bubbles form around it quickly; if the bubbles are out of control and smoky, it's too hot. If they are slow to form, the oil may need more heat or just a little more time. You can also use a wooden spoon: dunk in the handle and if bubbles quickly surround it, the oil is ready.

Cranberry Relish

> 2 cups fresh cranberries, coarsely chopped
> ½ cup pure maple syrup
> ½ cup water
> ¼ cup fresh orange juice
> 1 teaspoon finely grated orange zest

Mix together all ingredients in a small saucepan. Cover and bring to a boil. Once boiling, uncover and let simmer for 15 minutes. Bring to room temperature and serve.

VEGAN WITH A VENGEANCE

Seitan

In traditional seitan, the wheat flour is washed and kneaded three times over two days in order to develop the wheat gluten. I speed things up in this recipe by using vital wheat gluten flour. The flavoring for this goes well with pretty much anything, but depending what you are using it for you can change the flavors a bit by adding finely chopped herbs. Or, if you're making something Asian or Indian, some grated ginger would be nice. The first time I made seitan I used a recipe from the book Vegan Vittles. This recipe was inspired by that one, but has been modified over the years to make it even more awesome.

2 cups vital wheat gluten flour

¼ cup nutritional yeast

2 tablespoons all-purpose flour

1 cup cold water or vegetable broth

½ cup soy sauce

1 tablespoon tomato paste

1 tablespoon olive oil

2 cloves garlic, pressed or grated on a Microplane grater

1 teaspoon finely grated lemon zest

BROTH

12 cups water or vegetable broth

½ cup soy sauce

In a large bowl, mix together vital wheat gluten flour, nutritional yeast, and all-purpose flour. In a separate bowl, mix together the wet ingredients through the lemon zest.

Pour the wet ingredients into the dry and combine with a firm spatula. Knead the dough for about 5 minutes until spongy and elastic. Let the dough rest for a couple of minutes. In the meantime, stir together the ingredients for the broth in a large saucepot (do not boil the broth at this point).

Roll the dough into a log shape about 10 inches long and cut it into 6 pieces of roughly equal size. Place the pieces in the broth. It is important that the broth be very cold when you add the dough, which makes for a nicer texture and ensures that the seitan doesn't fall apart. Partially cover the pot (leave a little space for steam to escape) and bring the broth to a boil.

When the broth has come to a boil, set the heat to low and gently simmer for an hour, turning the pieces every now and again.

VEGAN WITH VENGEANCE

Turn off the heat and let the broth and seitan cool for at least a 30 minutes. This will produce a firmer seitan. It is best to let everything cool completely before removing the seitan from the broth.

What you do next depends on the recipe you are using. If storing the seitan for later use, slice it into bite-size chunks, put it into a sealable container, and cover with broth. Seal the container and place it in the fridge for up to five days.

Jerk Seitan

My favorite Brooklyn soul food restaurant closed without warning one day and I was left pressing my face against the glass, hoping against hope that it might somehow open again but it never did. They served the best jerk sauce known to woman. There isn't that much in the way of vegetarian soul food in Brooklyn so I took matters into my own hands and came up with this dish that satisfies my cravings quite nicely. This is the sort of recipe you can really play around with to your tastes. I rely on dry spices and pantry staples that are easy to substitute; the lime can be subbed with 3 tablespoons of apple cider vinegar, the maple syrup can be subbed with sugar. If you have a serrano chile pepper you can use that instead of or in addition to cayenne. This dish is pretty spicy as is, so taste the sauce before deciding that you want more heat.

FOR THE MARINADE:
½ large white onion, coarsely chopped
2 cloves garlic, crushed
1½ tablespoons fresh ginger, chopped
3 tablespoons fresh lime juice
3 tablespoons soy sauce
2 tablespoons olive oil
2 tablespoons pure maple syrup
1 tablespoon dried thyme
1 teaspoon ground allspice
¼ teaspoon ground cinnamon
¼ teaspoon ground cayenne
1 teaspoon ground or freshly grated nutmeg

FOR THE SEITAN:
2 cups seitan, cut into thick strips
2 teaspoons olive oil
1 onion, thickly sliced (about 1 cup)
1 green bell pepper, seeded and thickly sliced

Prepare the marinade by pureeing all of the ingredients in a blender or food processor until relatively smooth. There will be some chunkiness but that's okay. Place the seitan in a shallow bowl and pour that marinade over it. Mix to coat. Cover and let marinate for an hour.

In a large skillet, sauté the onions and peppers in olive oil over medium-high heat

VEGAN WITH A
VENGEANCE

for 5 to 7 minutes, until the onions start to brown. Remove the seitan from the marinade and reserve the liquid. Sauté for 10 minutes, until the seitan has browned to your liking. Add the remaining marinade and cook for about 2 minutes to heat the sauce through.

Serve with Coconut Rice (page 109), sautéed greens, and baked sweet potatoes or roasted autumn vegetables; ladle the extra sauce over each serving.

The Web can be a big scary place. A Google search for "vegan" will give you roughly three million results. If you don't already have a comfortable vegetarian home online, or like my mom, you aren't Web savvy, here are a few places I think you will enjoy.

Communities

Veganporn.com is the creation of Toronto-based vegan Herman Thrust. The first thing you notice when you go there is the surprising absence of porn, but he got your attention, right? This is a great site to keep up to date on current events—from genetic engineering to cat hunting in Wisconsin, Veganporn has got it covered. Members get their own journals in which to post their musings and Herman pulls from these journals, adding his commentary to make an informative and insightful and often humorous blog on the home page.

Vegpeople.com is such a great community. I don't know how they did it but it's full of intelligent, articulate, and well-informed people. I highly recommend it for the newbies in need of vegan support. Sections run the gamut from vegan fitness to book reviews, plus a section just for teens.

Veggieboards.com is probably the largest vegetarian message board on the Web. Users discuss the usual veggie-related topics, but it's a great place to go to while away the hours discussing things like TV, music, and film with other veggies. The boards can get a bit juvenile at times, but there's always a good conversation going on.

Livejournal has a number of vegetarian communities you can join once you become a member. It works like this: you choose a username (I don't think that vegslut is taken) and your own journal space to post all the fascinating aspects of your life: what you ate that morning, the ridiculous thing a co-worker said, why you would rather be attacked by orcas than by cenobites, you know, just whatever is on your mind. Once you have signed up (it's free, but a paid account gives you more customizable features) you can join other communities and make online friends. Some of my favorite vegetarian communities are Vegancooking, where (surprise! surprise!) you can get info on all things vegan and food. It's especially helpful if you need advice on egg replacers or want to know the easiest way to slice a mango. Veganfoodpics is a great place to post pictures of your dinner and have people care. Cheapvegan is a community for the zine of the same name where you can get helpful cooking hints for the budget-minded.

Blogs

If you don't already know, blog is short for "Web log." Cute, huh? There are millions of them and they can be fly-by-night. It's hard to sort the good from the bad, but here are a few that I check regularly.

Vegblog.org is Ryan MacMichael's account of his vegan journey. Well, it's not all so dramatic as that. Follow Ryan as he tackles recipes, reviews vegan products, discusses life as an animal rights activist, and provides analysis of vegetarianism in pop culture.

Veganfreaks.org is a relatively new site but became a fast favorite for me because our gregarious hosts Pleather and Vegannaise's posts are always so full of insight, information, and that darn critical thought that the kids love so much these days. A visit to Veganfreaks always leaves me thinking for at least a couple of minutes, and in Internet time minutes equal months.

Food Fight Grocery (www.foodfightgrocery.com/) is the Web site for the Portland-based vegan store, but they have a great blog on the home page. Chad always seems to find the stupidest and most amusing stuff, so I make sure to check their site every day, even when I don't need vegan haggis.

Recipes

Cooking with Chef Deb at **Vegsource.com** (www.vegsource.com/talk/recipes/index.html) is an incredible message board where you can ask Chef Deb anything related to cooking and get an answer that day. Looking for a vegan trifle? Want to know the cooking time for Brussels sprouts? Chef Deb is the one to ask.

PakuPaku (www.pakupaku.info/) doesn't have a ton of recipes, but every single one is delicious and vegan, including a wonderful section of Ethiopian yumminess.

Recipezaar isn't a vegetarian site, but do a search for "vegan" and you will get hundreds of results. What I like about this site is that the reviewers are usually pretty accurate, so you won't end up with a dud.

Seitan-Portobello Stroganoff

If you've been let down by vegan stroganoffs in the past let it go here and now; this dish will cure what ails you. The sauce has a rich "depth of flavor" and is bursting with creamy mushroomy goodness. I make my own seitan for this and I recommend that you do, too; it tastes better and is much, much less expensive. If you do make your own, then have it ready to be sautéed in the cast iron by the time you start the stroganoff. If you use store-bought seitan you may want to use a little less than the 3½ cups called for because it is so expensive. Supplement it with extra noodles and peas. This recipe makes a lot, so you may have plenty of yummy leftovers. Use it in a sammich the next day!

2 tablespoons arrowroot powder (cornstarch or potato starch will work, too)
2 cups cold water or vegetable broth
8 teaspoons olive oil
1 cup shallots, thinly sliced
1 large onion, quartered and sliced into half moons
3 cloves garlic, minced
2 cups cremini mushrooms, thinly sliced
2 portobello caps, thinly sliced
2 tablespoons fresh thyme, chopped
3½ cups seitan, sliced into thin, wide strips
2 teaspoons salt
1 cup Burgundy cooking wine
1 tablespoon Hungarian paprika
½ cup nutritional yeast
½ cup plain soy milk (I use Vitasoy)
2 teaspoons Dijon mustard
1 cup frozen green peas
½ pound wide noodles (I use Eden Farms' parsley-lemon strips or fettuccine or
   linguine broken in half), prepared according to the package directions

Dissolve the arrowroot in the 2 cups of water; set aside.

Heat 2 tablespoons of the olive oil in a skillet over medium-high heat. Add the shallots and onions, sauté for 5 minutes. Add the garlic, cremini and portobello mushrooms, and thyme. Sauté for 15 minutes.

Meanwhile, heat a cast-iron skillet with the remaining 2 teaspoons of olive oil, just long enough to coat it. Add the seitan and sauté over medium heat about 25 minutes, until it is dark brown and crispy on the outside. If you are using store-bought seitan you need only cook it for 10 minutes.

VEGAN WITH VENGEANCE

Back to the sauce: add the salt, wine, and paprika. Turn up heat to high to reduce the liquid, about 10 minutes.

Lower heat to medium-high, add the arrowroot mixture, stir well, and let the sauce thicken, about 5 minutes. Add the nutritional yeast and mix well until it is dissolved. Add the soy milk and mustard and bring heat down to low; be very careful not to let it boil now because it can make the soy milk and mustard bitter. Add the seitan and peas; cook for 10 more minutes.

Divide the noodles into bowls and mix with the stroganoff. It is best to mix immediately so that the pasta doesn't stick. You can top it off with tofu sour cream, but I like it just the way it is.

Cold Udon Noodles with Peanut Sauce and Seitan

Mmmm. I often get a dish like this on Allen Street on the Lower East Side at a vegan restaurant called Tien Garden. Temperature is important here to get the right taste sensations. The noodles and vegetables should be cold as can be, the sauce should be at room temperature, and the seitan should be warm. If you follow the directions you should have no problemo getting it all right. If you aren't serving immediately and the peanut sauce has been refrigerated, let the sauce sit out till it's at room temperature.

FOR THE PEANUT SAUCE:
2 teaspoons peanut oil
2 cloves minced garlic
2 tablespoons minced ginger
1 cup water
2 tablespoons soy sauce
1 teaspoon ground coriander
⅔ cup smooth all-natural peanut butter
2 tablespoons pure maple syrup
3 tablespoons rice vinegar
2 teaspoons Asian chile sauce (available in the Asian section of most grocery stores; hot sauce is an okay substitution)

FOR THE SEITAN:
1 pound seitan (2 cups) sliced into thin (¼-inch) strips
1 tablespoon peanut oil
1 clove garlic
2 teaspoons soy sauce

TO SERVE:
10 ounces udon noodles
¼ cup black sesame seeds (optional)
1 seedless cucumber, halved across, sliced into matchsticks
4 cups mung bean sprouts
1 red bell pepper, thinly sliced
2 cups scallions, chopped
Several lime wedges for serving

VEGAN WITH A
VENGEANCE

Make the peanut sauce:

In a small saucepan, sauté the garlic and ginger in peanut oil over low-medium heat. Add the water, soy sauce, and coriander and bring to a boil. Add the peanut butter and turn the heat to low. Whisk well until the peanut butter and oil are combined. Mix in the maple syrup, vinegar, and chile sauce. Remove from heat and let cool to room temperature.

Make the noodles:

Meanwhile, prepare your udon noodles according to the package directions. When noodles have cooked, drain them in a colander and rinse them under cold water until they are cool to the touch. Let them rest in the colander and prepare the seitan.

Sauté the seitan slices in the peanut oil for 5 minutes on each side or until the seitan is browned and yummy. Then sauté with the garlic for a minute, sprinkle with the soy sauce, and sauté again for 30 seconds or so.

At this point, your peanut sauce should be at room temperature. Give the noodles a final rinse under cold water to make them cold and also to keep them from sticking together.

To serve:

To serve, place the noodles on a large platter. Pour the peanut sauce over the noodles, then sprinkle with sesame seeds. Scatter the cucumbers, bean sprouts, and peppers on top, followed by the scallions. Place the warm seitan on top and place lime wedges around the circumference and gosh darn it you've got yourself a fine-looking meal. If you would prefer to serve on individual plates to keep the greedy people from stealing all the seitan then just follow the directions dividing everything among four to six plates.

Ethiopian Seitan and Peppers

New York has some great Ethiopian restaurants but it can't compare to Philly and DC and I make sure to stop in and eat with my hands whenever I'm traveling. Whenever I tell New Yorkers this they immediately get defensive and begin listing the same two restaurants, as if giving up props to another city might cost us something. Ethiopian food is usually served with injera, but Savory Crepes (page 177) make an easy substitution or you can serve over rice.

FOR THE PUREE:

6 serrano chiles, seeded and coarsely chopped (see Punk Points, page 61)

1 tablespoon fresh ginger, chopped

2 cloves garlic, crushed

1 teaspoon ground cumin

¼ teaspoon ground cardamom

¼ teaspoon ground turmeric

¼ teaspoon ground cloves

¼ teaspoon ground cinnamon

½ cup red wine

3 tablespoons olive oil

TO PREPARE THE SEITAN AND PEPPERS:

2 pounds homemade seitan (page 157), (it should be about 4 cups), cut into
2 × ½-inch strips

2 green bell peppers, seeded and cut into 1-inch strips

Preheat oven to 400°F.

Place all the puree ingredients in a blender and puree until relatively smooth.

Place the seitan strips and peppers in a 9 × 13-inch (preferably glass) baking dish; smother with the puree. Cover with foil and bake for 20 minutes. Remove the foil, flip the seitan and peppers, and cook for 20 more minutes. Serve with rice and vegetables.

ENTREES

VEGAN WITH VENGEANCE

Kabocha Squash Stuffed with Butternut Vindaloo

Vindaloo is a spicy sweet-and-sour curry. Naturally sweet butternut squash tastes great in this and mellows out the spiciness. If you don't want to stuff the squashes you can just make the stew and serve over rice.

3 tablespoons peanut oil
2 cups diced yellow onion
3 cloves garlic, minced
2 tablespoons grated ginger
1 tablespoon mustard seeds
1 tablespoon ground cumin
½ teaspoon ground cloves
4 cardamom pods
2 cinnamon sticks
¼ cup red wine vinegar
½ cup red wine
1 (12-ounce) can crushed tomatoes
1½ pounds Yukon gold potatoes, peeled and cut into ½-inch chunks
1½ pounds butternut squash, cut into ½-inch chunks
6 medium-size kabocha squashes
¼ cup pure maple syrup
Fresh chopped cilantro to garnish

In a stockpot over moderate heat, sauté the onions in oil for 5 to 7 minutes. Add the garlic and ginger; sauté until fragrant (about a minute); add all the seeds and spices and stir; add the red wine vinegar, red wine, and tomatoes. Mix to combine. Add the potatoes and butternut squash, cover, and bring to a low boil. Cook until potatoes are tender, about 25 minutes. Meanwhile, prepare the kabocha squashes.

Preheat oven to 375°F. Lightly grease a rimmed baking sheet. Cut off the top of the kabocha squashes and remove the seeds. Scrape inside with a tablespoon to remove the stringy parts. Cut a small sliver off the bottom of each squash so that you will later be able to stand the squash upright to stuff it. Place the squashes cut side down on the baking sheet, and bake for about 40 minutes. The squashes should be very soft and easily pierced with a fork.

Back to the stew: When potatoes are tender, add the maple syrup and heat through. Cover and keep warm until the squashes are ready.

Remove the squash from oven and, when cool enough to handle, stuff each with some of the stew. Garnish with cilantro and serve.

VEGAN WITH
VENGEANCE

Chickpea and Spinach Curry

I pretty much live on curries. I can't think of any other dish that packs so much flavor with so little work. I love tomato-based curries, and here the tomatoes are a pleasant backdrop and a sturdy base that isn't screaming tomato, so the spices can really shine through. It doesn't hurt that a tomato base has considerably less fat than, say, coconut milk, if you care about that sort of thing. Make sure your mustard seeds are visibly popping before adding the onions; if you've never cooked your own mustard seeds before, you are in for a treat that will change your curry making for good.

1 (12-ounce) can whole tomatoes (in juice, not puree)

3 tablespoons vegetable oil

2 teaspoons mustard seeds

1 large onion, cut into ¼-inch dice (about 2 cups)

4 cloves garlic, minced

2 tablespoons fresh ginger, minced

3 teaspoons curry powder

2 teaspoons ground cumin

1 teaspoon ground coriander

⅛ teaspoon ground cloves

½ teaspoon ground cinnamon

¼ teaspoon asafoetida (optional)

3 cardamom pods

1 teaspoon salt

10 cups fresh spinach, well rinsed and chopped

4 cups chickpeas, cooked and drained, or 2 (15-ounce) cans, drained and rinsed

Prepare the tomatoes by removing them one at a time from the can, squeezing out the juice, and tearing them into bite-size pieces. Place the prepared tomatoes in a bowl and reserve the juice in the can.

Preheat a medium-size saucepan over moderate heat; pour in the vegetable oil and then the mustard seeds. Let the seeds pop for about a minute (you may want to cover the pot so that the seeds can't escape), then add the onion; turn up the heat to medium-high and sauté for 7 to 10 minutes, until the onion begins to brown. Add garlic and ginger, and sauté 2 more minutes. Add spices, salt and ¼ cup of the reserved tomato juice; sauté one minute more. Add tomatoes and heat through. Add handfuls of spinach, mixing each addition until wilted. When all the spinach has completely wilted and the mixture is liquid-y, add the chickpeas. Lower the heat, cover, and simmer for 10 more minutes, stirring occasionally. Taste, and adjust the spices if necessary. Simmer uncovered for about 10 more minutes, or until a thick, stewlike consistency is achieved.

Fizzle says:

Asafoetida, also called hing powder, is root resin used in small doses in many Indian dishes. It's a little hard to find; you may need to go to a spice store, so it is optional in this recipe. If you can find it though, you will fall in love with its aromatic scent and flavor.

VEGAN WITH A VENGEANCE

Green Thai Curry

Making your own chile paste is easy and flavorful. While admittedly you won't be saving money by not purchasing the chile paste in a jar, you will embark on a culinary adventure that makes it worth it: the taste of homemade chile paste is just incomparable. There are several steps here but you should be able to have dinner on the table within an hour provided your tofu is already pressed. This is a great dish to serve a date, alongside the Fresh Mango Summer Rolls (page 84) and some jasmine rice.

FOR THE CHILE PASTE:
2 small Thai green peppers or serrano chiles, seeded and chopped
2 jalapeño peppers, seeded and chopped
½ cup boiling water
2 teaspoons crushed coriander seeds
1 teaspoon cumin seeds
5 white peppercorns (black peppercorns are an okay substitution)
1 tablespoon fresh chopped lemongrass (see Punk Points on next page)
1 tablespoon chopped fresh ginger (or galangal if you can find it)
3 cloves garlic
1 cup lightly packed fresh cilantro, plus extra for garnish
2 teaspoons finely grated lime zest
1 cup shallots, chopped

EVERYTHING ELSE:
5 tablespoons peanut oil
1 block tofu, pressed and cut into small triangles (page 144)
1 red bell pepper, seeded and thinly sliced
1 medium-size red onion, sliced into thin half moons
1 (15-ounce) can coconut milk
1½ tablespoons pure maple syrup
Juice of 1 lime
½ cup lightly packed fresh basil (Thai basil if you can find it)

To make the chili paste:

Place the serranos and jalapeños in a bowl, cover with about ½ cup boiling water, and let sit for 15 minutes.

Place the coriander seeds, cumin seeds, and peppercorns in a small skillet and toast over medium heat for about 2 minutes, until they are fragrant. Transfer to a food processor and grind into a powder. (If you are using a blender instead, it

VEGAN WITH A VENGEANCE

may not grind the seeds into a powder, it may just bounce them around, so either use a mortar and pestle or a coffee grinder to grind them or just place them with all the other ingredients and hope for the best.) Add the remaining ingredients, including the chiles in their water; grind to a paste. Cover and set aside until ready to use.

Heat 2 tablespoons of the peanut oil in a large nonstick skillet over medium-high heat. Add the tofu triangles and heat on each side until golden brown (about 4 minutes per side). Transfer to a large plate and cover with foil to keep warm. In the same skillet, sauté the red pepper and onions (add a little extra oil if needed) for about 3 minutes, until just slightly tender.

Preheat a heavy-bottomed medium-size saucepan over low-medium heat. Add the chile paste and cook for about 2 minutes, stirring constantly. Add the coconut milk and turn the heat up a bit. Mix together until the paste is incorporated; bring to a low boil. Add the maple syrup and lime juice, taste for sweetness, then add a little more maple syrup if necessary. Place the tofu, peppers, and onions in the sauce and cover; cook for 5 minutes. Add the basil and turn off the heat. Let sit for 5 minutes or so before serving. Transfer to serving bowls and garnish with fresh cilantro.

PUNK POINTS

Lemongrass looks sort of like a long stalk of bamboo but the only part you actually use is the heart of the stalk. You'll have to cut off the rest where the leaves start to branch and discard that, then peel off the rough outer leaves. The remaining "heart" can then be diced with a sharp knife.

VEGAN WITH A VENGEANCE

The Post Punk Kitchen is Brooklyn's fastest growing vegetarian punk rock cooking show because it's the only one. It is a "Bam!"-free space for vegetarians and food-lovers everywhere that came into being in 2003, born out of frustration over the garbage that the Food Network was trying to feed the masses (no pun intended). We believe that the airwaves and the risotto are for the people, not for corporations trying to peddle their processed-cheese wares. And we just really, really, really could not take another second of Rachael Ray saying "EVOO".

—From the PPK mission statement

When I started doing *The Post Punk Kitchen* I had this idea that if everyone started their own shows then pretty soon we would fill the public airwaves with quality TV for the people.

Public access varies from state to state but generally you pay a small fee to take a class that allows you to become a producer. The class should teach you very basic editing, filming, and lighting skills, but most importantly it allows you to use the station's equipment and facilities free of charge. With the help of other members you produce your show and you help them with theirs; eventually a star is born. It's such a great outlet for us little people to get our views and visions out there; take advantage of it. Start a radical gardening show, make a documentary about your pet snail, make a six-episode special about your grandma—the airwaves are ours!

Sweet Potato Crepes with Cilantro-Tamarind Sauce

SERVES 6

Terry and I made these for The Post Punk Kitchen's Valentine's Day episode (or rather, the anti-Valentine's Day episode) because they are sexy. The slightly sweet and aromatic filling wrapped in a warm chickpea crepe and smothered in a rich yet delicate sauce is sure to impress. We toasted our own spices to bring extra-fresh flavor to the curried sweet potatoes, but if you don't want to go the extra mile, even though you really should, then you can use ground spices.

1 recipe crepes (recipe follows)
2 teaspoons cumin seeds
1 teaspoon coriander seeds
1 teaspoon fenugreek seeds
1 teaspoon mustard seeds
2 cardamom pods
6 whole cloves
Pinch of ground cinnamon
Pinch of ground cayenne pepper
½ teaspoon salt

FOR THE FILLING:
2 tablespoons peanut oil
1½ cups yellow onion, finely chopped
1 red bell pepper, finely chopped
2 cloves garlic, minced
2 tablespoons grated ginger
2½ pounds sweet potatoes, peeled and chopped into ½-inch chunks
Half a (15-ounce) can coconut milk
1 tablespoon pure maple syrup
1 tablespoon fresh lime juice

FOR THE SAUCE:
½ cup raw cashews
2 cups lightly packed fresh cilantro
2 teaspoons tamarind concentrate
Half a (15-ounce) can coconut milk

VEGAN WITH
VENGEANCE

1 teaspoon pure maple syrup
1 tablespoon peanut oil
Pinch salt

To prepare the spice blend:

Heat a small skillet over medium heat. Pour in all of the seeds, pods, and cloves except for the cinnamon and cayenne, and toast for about 3 minutes, shaking the skillet back and forth for even heating. The spices should smell warm and toasty. Remove the mixture from the pan immediately and transfer to a bowl to cool. When fully cooled, place in a spice grinder (a coffee grinder works) or mortar and pestle. Grind to a fine powder and add the cinnamon, cayenne, and salt. Set aside.

To prepare the filling:

Preheat a large skillet oven moderate heat. Pour in the oil and heat, then add the onions and bell pepper, and sauté for about 5 minutes. Add the garlic and ginger; sauté about 2 minutes more. Add the spice blend and make sure the onions are coated with it. Add the sweet potatoes and cook for a minute or two. Cover the pan and cook for 15 more minutes, stirring frequently, until the sweet potatoes are tender. (You should prepare the sauce while they are cooking). Add the coconut milk, maple syrup, and lime juice, cover, and cook for 5 more minutes, stirring occasionally. The coconut milk should be fully incorporated into the sweet potatoes.

To prepare the sauce:

Grind the cashews in a blender or food processor. Add the remaining ingredients and blend until smooth. That's it!

To Assemble:

There should be two crepes per plate. Place one crepe on a plate, fill with about ½ cup of filling and fold each side over, like a jacket. Repeat with a second crepe and drizzle with tamarind sauce.

VEGAN WITH A VENGEANCE

Savory Crepes

MAKES 12 CREPES

This is Terry's recipe from when she worked in a vegan restaurant. Don't worry if your first crepe isn't perfect; even pros tear a crepe or two from time to time. Just move on to the next one.

> 1½ cups all-purpose unbleached flour
> ½ cup chickpea flour
> 1 teaspoon salt
> 2 tablespoons olive oil
> 2 cups water

Combine the flours and salt in a medium-size mixing bowl. Make a well in the center of the flour and add the water and olive oil. Use an electric hand mixer to blend until completely smooth (if you don't have a mixer, mix with a fork for a good solid 3 minutes). Cover the batter with plastic wrap and let chill in the fridge for ½ hour or so.

Preheat your crepe pan or a nonstick skillet that is 8 inches or so across. Spray the pan with nonstick cooking spray or a very thin layer of olive oil. Pour ¼ cup of batter into the pan; tilt and rotate the pan so that the crepe batter has covered the bottom and crept up the sides of the pan just a tiny bit. When it looks like the top of the crepe has pretty much set and the corners of the crepes are just beginning to brown, flip over with a spatula and cook the other side for just under a minute.

You can remove the crepe in one of two ways (and probably more than two but this is how I do it: (1) fold the crepe in half and then in half again, so that it's folded into a triangular shape; or (2) use a spatula to transfer the crepe to a large plate, putting a sheet of waxed paper between each crepe to keep them from sticking. You may be able to get away with not using the waxed paper if you'd like to chance it. Either way you do it, cover the plate with foil as you make the remainder of the crepes.

VEGAN WITH A VENGEANCE

Moroccan Tagine with Spring Vegetables

Tagine **is the** name of the traditional clay pot used by Moroccans to produce flavorful and aromatic stews and other dishes. The name was carried over in America to include stews made with spices often used in Moroccan cooking. Or so they tell me. This is a deliciously spiced stew that I'm sure they don't actually serve in Morocco but what the hell. It's packed full of vegetables and lentils, making it a veritable powerhouse of nutrition. Serve over couscous.

2 tablespoons olive oil

2 medium onions, quartered and sliced thin

1 cup baby carrots, cut into ¼–inch dice

1 serrano chile, seeded and minced, to taste (see Punk Points, page 61)

3 cloves garlic, minced

2 tablespoons grated fresh ginger

2 teaspoons ground cumin

1 teaspoon ground turmeric

1 teaspoon ground coriander

2 cups vegetable stock

3 cups water

2 tablespoons tomato paste

2 cinnamon sticks

2 bay leaves

Several dashes fresh black pepper

1 cup dried red lentils, washed

1 zucchini, halved lengthwise and sliced ¼ inch thick

1 cup green beans, cut into 1-inch pieces

2 cups grape tomatoes, halved

½ cup raisins

1 teaspoon salt

1 bunch spinach, torn into pieces (4 cups)

½ cup chopped cilantro leaves

½ cup chopped mint

Lemon wedges to serve

VEGAN WITH A VENGEANCE

In a stockpot, sauté the onions in the olive oil over medium heat for 3 minutes. Add the carrots and chile and sauté 3 minutes more. Add the garlic and ginger; sauté for 2 minutes. Add the cumin, turmeric, and coriander, and mix. Add the stock, water, tomato paste, cinnamon sticks, bay leaves, black pepper, and lentils. Bring to a boil, then lower heat and simmer, uncovered, for 20 minutes.

Add the veggies (except the spinach) and raisins and salt, simmer 15 more minutes. Add the spinach, cilantro, and mint; stir well. When the spinach has wilted completely (about 1 minute), turn the heat off. Let the stew sit for 10 minutes. Remove the bay leaves and cinnamon sticks. Serve over couscous with plenty of lemon wedges to squeeze in.

VEGAN WITH VENGEANCE

Brooklyn Pad Thai

Is this authentic? Most assuredly not, but it does taste a lot like the pad thai served every two feet here in Brooklyn. When making pad thai you have to make it only two servings at a time or the noodles will get mushy and the sauce won't be well distributed. This recipe is to serve four so you'll need to divide the ingredients between each cooking session. Once everything is prepared the actual cooking is only about 3 to 4 minutes, so everyone can still eat together. I use tongs to mix everything; they make it easier to not mush up the noodles.

1 pound rice noodles

FOR THE SAUCE:
6 tablespoons tamari
6 tablespoons sugar
2 tablespoons tomato paste
2 tablespoons Asian hot chile sauce or hot sauce
¼ cup rice wine vinegar
3 tablespoons tamarind concentrate or lime juice

FOR THE PAD THAI:
6 tablespoons peanut oil
1 pound tofu, drained and pressed cut into small triangles (page 144)
1 medium-size red onion, cut in half and thinly sliced
2 cloves garlic, minced
1 tablespoon finely minced lemongrass
2 cups bean sprouts
8 scallions, sliced into 1½-inch lengths
2 small dried red chiles, crumbled
½ cup chopped roasted peanuts
¼ cup chopped fresh cilantro
Lime wedges for serving

Prepare the rice noodles according to the package directions.

Mix together the ingredients for the sauce.

Preheat a large nonstick skillet or wok over moderate-high heat. Pour 2 tablespoons of the peanut oil into the pan and heat, then quickly add the tofu. Stir-fry for 4 to 5 minutes, until the tofu is crisp on the outside. Remove from pan and set aside.

Pour 2 tablespoons more of the peanut oil into the pan. Add half the red onion and stir-fry for 30 seconds. Add half the garlic and half the lemongrass, and stir-fry for 30 more seconds. Add half of the sauce and, when it starts to bubble (should bubble within a few seconds), add half the noodles. Cook for 2 minutes, stirring constantly, then add half the tofu, bean sprouts, scallions, chiles, and peanuts. Stir for 30 more seconds. Transfer to two serving plates and garnish with cilantro and lime wedges. Repeat with the remaining ingredients.

VEGAN WITH
VENGEANCE

Millet and Spinach Polenta with Sun-dried Tomato Pesto

I got the idea for millet polenta from a fabulous book called The Splendid Grain. It's easier to prepare than polenta made with the traditional cornmeal because it doesn't require as much stirring and attention. This is a yummy version, flecked with spinach and oregano and topped with a savory Sundried Tomato Pesto. Toasting the millet beforehand brings out its nutty flavor.

> 1 cup millet
> 3 cups vegetable stock
> 1 tablespoon olive oil plus more for cooking the polenta
> 2 cups shredded fresh spinach, well rinsed
> 1 tablespoon chopped fresh oregano
> ½ teaspoon salt
> A few dashes fresh black pepper
> Sun-dried Tomato Pesto (page 183)

Toast the millet in a dry skillet for about 5 minutes over high heat, stirring constantly until the millet releases a nutty aroma. Rinse in a fine-mesh sieve or a large bowl, until the water runs clear; drain as best you can.

Bring the millet, vegetable broth, and olive oil to a boil in a saucepan. Lower heat and simmer for about 25 minutes. Mix in the spinach, oregano, salt, and pepper; simmer 10 more minutes, uncovered, until all the liquid is absorbed.

You have a few options for molding your polenta; it all depends on the shape that you want.

For squares or rectangles:

Lightly grease a lidded plastic container that is roughly 11 × 7 inches. Spread the polenta into the container and let cool on the countertop. When fully cooled, cut into desired size rectangles.

For circles:

Lightly grease two 16-ounce tin cans or three 12-ounce juice concentrate containers. Spoon the polenta into the containers and pack tightly; let cool on the countertop. When fully cooled, remove the polenta from the containers and cut into 1-inch slices. Note: It may take up to 2 hours for the polenta to get firm

VEGAN WITH A VENGEANCE

enough to cool in the cans. If you try to remove it before then, it will break and you will be sad. You may also need to drag a thin knife around the circumference to loosen the polenta. The juice concentrate containers are a great deal easier to unmold: you can jiggle them upside down until the polenta loosens and comes out. If it won't budge, rip or cut the edge of the container with scissors and unravel it as necessary.

Prepare the polenta:

Preheat a large skillet over moderate heat for a minute or two. Coat the pan with a very thin layer of olive oil; fry the polenta on each side for 3 minutes. Serve immediately, topped with Sun-dried Tomato Pesto, and with roasted asparagus on the side.

Sun-dried Tomato Pesto

MAKES ABOUT 1½ CUPS

This was submitted to my site by Frannie and I modified it a bit because I can't leave well enough alone. It's great as a pizza or pasta topping or on the Millet and Spinach Polenta.

> ½ cup tightly packed sun-dried tomatoes
> 1 cup water
> ¼ cup almonds
> 2 cloves garlic, chopped
> 2 tablespoons olive oil
> ¼ teaspoon salt
> A few dashes fresh black pepper
> ¼ cup chopped fresh basil

Place the sun-dried tomatoes in a saucepan and cover with water. Bring to a low boil, then turn the heat off and let soak for about 15 minutes, until soft.

Grind the almonds in a blender or food processor. Add the sun-dried tomatoes (with the water), garlic, olive oil, salt, and pepper, and puree.

Transfer to a bowl and stir in the basil. Let sit for a few minutes to allow the flavors to blend.

VEGAN WITH A
VENGEANCE

Revolutionary Spanish Omelet with Saffron and Roasted Red Pepper— Almond Sauce

This is another wonderful recipe from Terry, and even though it's an omelet it makes a great entrée. She tells us, "If the anarchist revolutionaries in the Spanish Civil War had known about the magic of tofu they would have made a traditional dish just like this. Or maybe it's just my hopes for an egalitarian, nonauthoritarian society talking again. Known in Spain simply as a 'tortilla' the thick, oven-baked omelet of eggs, potatoes, onions, and olive oil is found in virtually every café and can be eaten at any meal any time of day. Below is a liberatingly egg-free version—with the addition of saffron—that bakes up a beautiful golden yellow with the delicate flavor of the classic Spanish spice. The flavors improve with time so you can make it the night before and serve cold or at room temperature. Along with a dollop of Roasted Red Pepper–Almond Sauce and crusty bread this tortilla of the Revolution is a sturdy meal that will carry you through many an anarcho-syndicalist collective workers' meeting."

A small pinch saffron threads
3 tablespoons plain soy milk
¼ cup plus 1 tablespoon olive oil, plus extra for spraying omelet
1 medium-size onion, peeled, halved and thinly sliced
4 medium-size Yukon gold potatoes, unpeeled, halved and sliced into ¼-inch
    slices (make sure they're all the same thickness to ensure even cooking)
1½ pounds soft tofu, drained
2 cloves garlic, crushed
1 teaspoon salt
Dash of cayenne pepper

Place the saffron threads in a small cup and gently press the threads with the back of a spoon a few times; don't crush completely. Warm the soy milk in a small saucepan till just about boiling. Remove from heat and pour over the saffron; stir briefly and set aside for a minimum of 25 minutes. The longer the saffron soaks in the soy milk, the more flavor and color will be released.

Preheat oven to 375°F. Pour ¼ cup of the olive oil into a 10-inch cast-iron skillet. Add the sliced potatoes and onions. The pan should not be completely full; there should be about ¼ inch of space left on top; remove some potatoes if it appears too

VEGAN WITH A VENGEANCE

full. Gently toss the onions and potatoes in oil to coat. Place in the oven and roast for 30 to 35 minutes, stirring on occasion, till onions are very soft and the potatoes are tender.

Meanwhile, in a food processor blend till smooth the drained tofu, garlic, and remaining 1 tablespoon of olive oil. Strain the soy milk mixture with a fine-mesh sieve (if you're superthrifty you can save the saffron threads, dry them, and use once more) and add to tofu mixture along with salt and cayenne pepper. Blend till creamy.

When the potatoes and onions are tender, remove from oven. Pour the tofu mixture into the pan and gently fold the potatoes and onions into the tofu mixture. With a rubber spatula, smooth the top, making sure to make the center slightly more shallow than the outside; this will help ensure the center cooks evenly.

Spray the top of the omelet with olive oil and return to the oven. Bake for 50 minutes to 1 hour till the top is deep yellow and lightly browned in spots, and a knife inserted into the center comes out clean. Remove from oven and allow to cool at least 20 minutes before cutting.

To cut, run a knife along the edges, and press down on the omelet while slicing. To serve it real Spanish style you'll need to remove it whole from the pan: put a plate on top of the pan and with both hands securely holding pan and plate, flip the entire thing upside-down. Put on a countertop and gently remove the pan—the finished omelet is oily enough so most of it should slide easily onto the plate. If you preferred the golden yellow side to be on top, simply flip again onto another plate.

Excellent both warm and at room temperature. Serve as the Spanish do with ketchup (a good all-natural one worthy of revolutionaries) or with Roasted Red Pepper–Almond Sauce.

Roasted Red Pepper—Almond Sauce

> 3 red bell peppers, roasted, skinned, seeds removed, and torn into chunks
> ¼ cup almond meal or finely ground almonds
> 2 cloves garlic, peeled and crushed
> 3 tablespoons olive oil
> ¼ cup fresh squeezed lemon juice
> 1 teaspoon dried thyme
> 1½ teaspoons sugar
> Salt to taste

Blend all the ingredients in a food processor until thick and creamy. Makes about 1¼ cups.

VEGAN WITH VENGEANCE

Mushroom and Sun-dried Tomato Risotto

Risotto is a creamy rice dish that isn't difficult to make but does require a lot of maintenance; you need to stir it pretty much constantly. Try to get your roommates or family to help with the stirring, although when I make it alone I just blast some music and go into a Zen-like trance, where it's just the risotto and me on a hillside in Italy. I added truffle oil as an optional ingredient because it can cost about $10 a bottle, but you need only a few drops to add a deep, earthy mushroom flavor and that bottle can definitely last you a year or more; compared to the price of actual truffles that's quite a bargain.

6 cups vegetable broth
1 cup dried shiitake mushrooms
3 tablespoons olive oil
1 cup finely chopped shallots
3 cups thinly sliced cremini mushrooms
¼ cup chopped sun-dried tomatoes
2 garlic cloves, minced
1 tablespoon minced fresh thyme
2 teaspoons minced fresh rosemary
½ teaspoon ground or freshly grated nutmeg
A few dashes fresh black pepper
½ teaspoon salt
1½ cups arborio rice
A few drops black truffle oil (optional)

Bring the broth to a simmer in a medium-size saucepan. Add the dried shiitake mushrooms and simmer for about 2 minutes, until the mushrooms are tender. Using a slotted spoon, transfer the mushrooms to a plate. When cool enough to handle, coarsely chop them. Cover the broth and keep warm over very low heat.

In a medium-size saucepan over moderate heat, sauté the shallots for about 5 minutes; add the cremini mushrooms and sun-dried tomatoes, and cook until mushrooms are tender and most of the moisture has been released, about 7 minutes. Add the garlic, shiitakes, herbs, spices, and salt; sauté another 3 minutes.

Add the rice and stir with a wooden spoon for 2 minutes. Add 1 cup of broth; stirring often, simmer until the liquid is absorbed, about 6 minutes. Continue to cook and stir, adding more broth by cupfuls, until the rice is tender and creamy and all the broth is absorbed. This should take about 30 minutes. Spoon onto plates and sprinkle some truffle oil over each serving if you like.

VEGAN WITH A
VENGEANCE

Eggplant and Artichoke alla Napoletana

This is bread crumb-coated eggplant layered with a Mediterranean artichoke "ragout" and smothered in Classic Pesto (page 132) and Sun-dried Tomato Pesto (page 183). You don't have to use artichokes; fresh zucchini makes a nice substitution. You need to use a lot of bowls and pans to make this, so don't say I didn't warn you. It's a cute little dish, though, and worth all the futzing.

FOR THE ARTICHOKE FILLING:

3 tablespoons extra-virgin olive oil

1 cup finely chopped chopped onion

2 garlic cloves, minced

½ teaspoon dried thyme

½ teaspoon salt

A few dashes fresh black pepper

8 plum tomatoes, diced

2 cups coarsely chopped artichoke hearts (if using canned, be sure to wash off any seasoning)

½ cup thinly sliced, pitted kalamata olives

¼ cup capers, drained

¼ cup chopped fresh basil

FOR THE EGGPLANT SLICES:

1 cup water

1 tablespoon cornstarch

1 cup all-purpose flour

1 cup panko

¼ teaspoon dried thyme

¼ teaspoon dried oregano

A few dashes fresh black pepper

½ teaspoon salt

1 large eggplant, sliced ¼ inch thick

Oil for frying

Prepare the artichokes:

In a large skillet over medium heat sauté the onions in the oil until translucent—about 3 minutes. Add the garlic and cook 1 minute more. Add the thyme, salt, pepper, and tomatoes and cook until the tomatoes have broken down and released their juices, about 5 minutes. Add the artichoke hearts, olives, and capers; simmer for 10 minutes. Add the basil and cook 1 minute more. Cover to keep warm.

Prepare the eggplant:

Have ready a flattened paper bag or paper towels to drain the oil.

In a broad bowl whisk the cornstarch with the water until dissolved. Fill a dinner plate with the flour. Onto another plate sift together the bread crumbs, spices, salt, and pepper. Line up the dishes as follows: flour, cornstarch mixture, panko.

Heat a little over ¼ inch of oil in a heavy-bottomed skillet over moderate heat. Dip an eggplant slice in the flour, then in the cornstarch mixture, and then in the breadcrumbs, flipping to coat. When you have dipped four slices use tongs to place them in the oil and cook until lightly browned, about 3 minutes. Flip over and cook 1 to 2 minutes more. Transfer to the paper to drain and proceed with the remaining eggplant slices.

PUNK POINTS

Some say that sprinkling eggplant with salt removed the bitterness, although I am not convinced it is a wholly necessary step since some eggplant is bred to be less bitter. If you would like to try it for yourself, sprinkle the eggplant slices with salt and set on paper towels for half an hour. Rinse the salt off of the eggplant, pat dry, and proceed with the recipe.

Assemble the layers:

Pour some of the sauce you are using onto the plate. Place an eggplant slice on the sauce, then a layer of the artichokes, then an eggplant slice, then another layer of the artichokes. Add one final eggplant slice and top with sauce.

VEGAN WITH A VENGEANCE

I **have a** thing against kitchen equipment that is shiny and new. I prefer the broken-in items that have been used and loved. Unfortunately, I found out the hard way that sometimes these things don't always love you back. In fact, they may electrocute you. My rule of thumb for buying used kitchen equipment is to avoid all things requiring electricity. Once an adorable waffle iron gave me the shock of my life and you would have thought I'd learned my lesson. But no, I just had to try a used blender, as well. It was from the '70s and the kind of avocado green that only existed in its pure form in that decade. The motor caught fire and the smoothie I was making flew hither and yon . . . it wasn't pretty.

My thrift-store utensils, however, have brought me much happiness. My handheld blender is unmatched in quality and design. I have a spatula that I use when cooking on cast iron. It is perfectly thin and wonderfully flexible, something I can't seem to find in anything from the box stores nowadays. Spatulas are some of the kitchen products I totally recommend buying used. (If the fact that you don't know where something has been appalls you, just soak the item in a little bleach and put your worries out of your mind.) The kind of quality that was standard back in the day doesn't have to cost you today's prices. Of course, sometimes used items are called "vintage" and cost ten times as much as they should, so I usually shop at the Salvation Army, Goodwill, or stoop and yard sales and avoid thrift stores that are too conscious of their kitsch appeal.

I defy you to show me one person that doesn't love a cookie. Whenever I want to say thank-you to people I bake them cookies, or I at least think of doing it. Sometimes I bake the cookies and just eat them myself and then send an e-mail with dancing bunnies to thank the people instead.

COOKIES AND BARS

Sparkled Ginger Cookies

Maybe these chewy, spicy sweet cookies are good any time of the year but I like to save them for the holidays. They make me nostalgic for the snowy winter days at grandma's cabin, sitting around the fireplace in our flannels singing . . . OK, fine, my grandma didn't have a cabin. There was no fireplace, no flannels, but these cookies sure make me wish there had been.

4 tablespoons turbinado or demerrara sugar (regular sugar will work as well but
  coarse is best)
2 cups all-purpose flour
1 teaspoon baking soda
¼ teaspoon salt
2½ teaspoons ground ginger
½ teaspoon ground cinnamon
½ teaspoon ground cloves
½ cup canola oil
¼ cup molasses
¼ cup soy milk
1 cup sugar
1 teaspoon vanilla extract

Preheat oven to 350°F. Lightly grease two cookie sheets. Place the turbinado sugar in a small bowl.

Sift together the flour, baking soda, salt, and spices. In a separate large mixing bowl, mix together the oil, molasses, soy milk, sugar, and vanilla. Pour the dry ingredients into the wet and combine well. Roll into 1-inch balls, flatten into a 1½-inch-diameter disk , press the cookie tops into the turbinado sugar and place 1 inch apart sugar side up on a prepared cookie sheet. Bake 10 to 12 minutes, let cool on cookie sheets for 3 to 5 minutes, transfer to cooling rack.

VEGAN WITH A VENGEANCE

Chocolate Chip Cookies

There's nothing healthy about these. I feel like I have to get that out of the way because sometimes people think vegan translates into healthy and although I usually try to make my cookies a little bit more healthy than your average cookie, I didn't even bother here. This cookie was made for the sole purpose of proving to someone I work with that my vegan cookies were just as good as his unvegan ones, and it worked!

1 cup nonhydrogenated margarine, at room temperature
1¼ cups sugar
1 tablespoon molasses
2 teaspoons vanilla extract
2½ cups all-purpose flour
1 teaspoon baking soda
1 teaspoon salt
1½ cups semisweet chocolate chips (I looove Tropical Source ones)

Preheat oven to 350°F.

Cream together the margarine and sugar until fluffy. Add the molasses and vanilla. Add the flour, baking soda, and salt, and mix well. Fold in the chocolate chips. Drop by teaspoonfuls spaced a little over 2 inches apart onto ungreased cookie sheets. Bake for 8 to 10 minutes, until ever so slightly browned. Let cool on the baking sheets for 5 minutes, then transfer to a cooling rack.

VEGAN WITH A VENGEANCE

Maple Walnut Cookies

When I first discovered maple extract you couldn't stop me from adding it to everything. These are buttery, chewy, and rich. It's a perfect way to celebrate National Vermont Day, if there were one.

½ cup canola oil

¼ cup pure maple syrup

2 tablespoons molasses

1 teaspoon vanilla extract

2 teaspoons maple extract

¾ cup sugar

¼ cup rice or soy milk

2 tablespoons tapioca starch or arrowroot or cornstarch

1½ cups all-purpose flour

¾ teaspoon salt

1 teaspoon baking soda

1½ cups chopped walnuts

3 dozen walnut halves

Preheat oven to 350°F. Lightly grease three cookie sheets or line them with parchment paper.

Combine the oil, maple syrup, molasses, vanilla and maple extracts, and sugar in a mixing bowl and stir until well combined. The oil will separate a little but that's okay. Add the soy milk and tapioca starch and mix until the tapioca is dissolved and the mixture resembles caramel.

Add the flour, salt, and baking soda. Mix with a wooden spoon until well combined. Fold in the chopped walnuts.

Drop by tablespoonfuls about 2 inches apart onto the prepared cookie sheets. Press a walnut half into the center of each cookie. Bake for 8 to 10 minutes. Remove from oven, let sit for 2 minutes, then transfer to a cooling rack.

VEGAN WITH A VENGEANCE

Get Rid of the Eggs

Replacing eggs is the most challenging aspect of vegan baking. Those suckers bind, they leaven, and they give structure to our baked goods. However, like a bad boyfriend, they can be replaced, and with pleasing results. Here's some info on replacements I have tried.

FLAXSEEDS

How to use:

1 tablespoon flaxseeds plus 3 tablespoons water replaces one egg. Finely grind 1 tablespoon whole flaxseeds in a blender or coffee grinder, or use 2 tablespoons pre-ground flaxseeds. Transfer to a bowl and beat in 3 tablespoons of water using a whisk or fork. It will become very gooey and gelatinous, much like an egg white. In some recipes, you can leave the ground flaxseeds in the blender and add the other wet ingredients to it, thus saving you the extra step of the bowl.

When it works best:

Flaxseeds have a distinct earthy granola-y taste. It tastes best and works very well in things like pancakes, and such whole-grain items such as bran or corn muffins. It is perfect for oatmeal cookies, and the texture works for cookies in general, although the taste may be too pronounced for some. Chocolate cake-y recipes have mixed results, I would recommend only using one egg's worth of flaxseed replacement in those, because the taste can be overpowering.

Tips:

Always store ground flaxseeds in the freezer because they are highly perishable. This mixture is not only an excellent replacement for eggs, it also contributes vital omega-3 fatty acids.

Where to get flaxseeds:

Health food stores

SILKEN TOFU

How to use it:

¼ cup blended silken tofu = 1 egg. Whiz in a blender until completely smooth and creamy, leaving no graininess or chunks. You will want to add other wet ingredients to this mixture to get it to blend properly. I recommend vacuum-packed extra-firm silken tofu, such as Mori-Nu.

When it works best:

Silken tofu works best in dense cakes and brownies, and in smaller quantities for lighter cakes and fluffy things (if the recipe calls for 3 eggs, use only 2 "tofu" eggs"). Whizzed tofu leaves virtually no taste, so it is an excellent replacer in delicate cake recipes where flaxseeds would overpower the flavor. In cookie recipes, it may make the cookie more cake-y and fluffy than anticipated, so add 1 teaspoon of starch (such as arrowroot or cornstarch) to the recipe to combat that. Silken tofu may make pancakes a little heavy, so it is not recommended for those, although it could work well with a little experimentation.

Where to get it:

Health food stores, and in some supermarkets (look in produce section).

ENER-G EGG REPLACER

How to use it:

1½ tablespoons Ener-G + 2 tablespoons water mixed well = 1 egg

Many people swear by this egg replacer. I think it is good to use in a pinch, in all baking that requires a few eggs. However, I can definitely taste it in cakes and cookies (tastes chalky), and I'm not crazy about the dense texture it turns out.

When it works best:

It seems to work best in cookies, or things that are supposed to be a little crispy.

Where to get it:

Health food stores, some supermarkets (look in baking or ethnic food section)

BANANA

How to use it:

½ banana blended until smooth or mashed well = 1 egg.

Bananas work wonders as an egg replacer in baking, which is the reason many banana bread recipes don't require eggs. They hold the air bubbles well, make things nice and moist, and impart a nice flavor. However, you don't want everything tasting like banana, so use in things where the taste won't be intrusive. I've also noticed that baked goods using banana brown very nicely, but sometimes you don't want your recipe to come out that brown.

VEGAN WITH A VENGEANCE

When it works best:

Quick breads, muffins, cakes, pancakes

Tip:

Make sure bananas are nice and ripe and have started to brown.

Where to get it:

Just kidding, I think you can figure this one out.

SOY YOGURT

How to use it:

¼ cup soy yogurt = 1 egg.

Soy yogurt works a lot like whizzed tofu as an egg replacer. It makes things moist and yummy.

When it works best:

Quick breads, muffins, cakes

Where to get it:

Health food stores, yuppyish supermarkets

Lose the Milk

This is a no-brainer. Use soy, rice, or almond milk. Buttermilk? Add a teaspoon of apple cider vinegar or lemon juice to your milk substitute and let it sit for a couple of minutes.

It's Like Buttah . . .

MARGARINE

Instead of butter try unsalted dairy-free margarine or go ahead and use salted but reduce the amount of salt in the recipe. Lose ¼ teaspoon of salt per ½ stick of margarine. But try to use the nonhydrogenated kind, I dunno, for your health?

OIL

My favorite thing to use instead of butter is canola oil, but you can use any vegetable oil; just reduce the amount. If a recipe calls for one stick of butter, which is ½ cup, I use ⅓ cup of oil.

Pumpkin Oatmeal Cookies

These are soft out of the oven, but as they cool they are nice and chewy. I use ground flaxseeds to make them a little chewier but it is an optional ingredient.

2 cups all-purpose flour
1⅓ cups rolled oats
1 teaspoon baking soda
¾ teaspoon salt
1 teaspoon cinnamon
½ teaspoon nutmeg
1⅔ cups sugar
⅔ cup canola oil
2 tablespoons molasses
1 cup canned pumpkin, or cooked pureed pumpkin (do not use pumpkin pie mix)
1 teaspoon vanilla extract
1 tablespoon ground flaxseeds (optional)
1 cup walnuts, finely chopped
½ cup raisins

Preheat oven to 350°F. Lightly grease two cookie sheets.

Mix together the flour, oats, baking soda, salt, and spices.

In a separate bowl, mix together the sugar, oil, molasses, pumpkin, and vanilla (and flaxseeds if using) until very well combined. Add the dry ingredients to the wet in three batches, folding to combine. Fold in the walnuts and raisins.

Drop by tablespoons onto the prepared cookie sheets. They don't spread very much so they can be placed only an inch apart. Flatten the tops of the cookies with a fork or with your fingers, to press into a cookie shape. Bake for 16 minutes at 350°F. If you are using two sheets of cookies on two levels of your oven, rotate the sheets halfway through for even baking. You'll have enough batter for four sheets.

Remove from oven, cool on the cookie sheets for 2 minutes, then transfer to a cooling rack. These taste best when they've had some time to cool and set. They taste even better the next day!

VEGAN WITH A VENGEANCE

Big Gigantoid Crunchy Peanut Butter–Oatmeal Cookies

Terry baked these for a Post Punk Kitchen bake sale, and they went flying off the table, luckily no one was hurt. They're really peanut buttery and satisfying.

2 cups all-purpose flour
2 cups rolled oats
2 teaspoons baking powder
1 teaspoon salt
¾ cup canola oil
¾ cup chunky all-natural peanut butter (salted is okay if you like a salty peanut butter flavor)
1 cup granulated sugar
1 cup brown sugar
½ cup vanilla soy milk
2 teaspoons vanilla extract

Preheat oven to 350°F. Lightly grease two cookie sheets.

Toss together the flour, oats, baking powder, and salt in a large mixing bowl. In a separate bowl mix together the oil, peanut butter, sugars, soy milk, and vanilla.

Add the dry ingredients to the wet, and mix. The dough will be very firm and moist. For perfectly round, large cookies: pack a ⅓-cup measuring cup with dough, pop out and roll the dough into a firm ball and flatten just barely on a prepared cookie sheet, spacing the dough balls well apart. Lightly grease the bottom of a glass or heavy ceramic pie plate; press the top of the cookies with the bottom of the pie plate to flatten to a ½-inch thickness. Leave about an inch between the flattened cookies as these will spread slightly. Bake for about 12 to 15 minutes till cookies have puffed a bit and are lightly browned. Allow to cool at least 10 minutes to firm up before moving off the cookie sheet. You can also make normal-size cookies using 1 to 2 tablespoons of dough instead, baking these 8 to 10 minutes.

199

COOKIES AND BARS

Crispy Peanut Butter Cookies

Cute, simple, crispy peanut butter cookies with a crosshatched top, perfect for munching on with a glass of soy milk.

⅓ cup canola oil
¾ cup brown sugar
1 cup all-natural, smooth, unsalted peanut butter
1 teaspoon vanilla extract
1 tablespoon cornstarch
1 cup flour
½ teaspoon baking powder
⅛ teaspoon salt

Preheat oven to 350°F. Lightly grease two cookie sheets.

In a mixing bowl, cream together the oil, sugar, peanut butter, and vanilla. Add the cornstarch and beat till well combined. Add the flour, baking powder, and salt; mix well.

Drop the dough by rounded tablespoonfuls about one inch apart onto a prepared cookie sheet and flatten each one a bit with the palm of your hand. Use the backside of a fork to press into each cookie, then press in the opposite direction to create a crosshatched pattern. Clean off the fork whenever it starts collecting too much dough. Bake for 12 minutes, let sit on the cookie sheets to cool for about 3 minutes, transfer to cooling rack to cool.

VEGAN WITH A VENGEANCE

Buttery Lemon Cutout Cookies

You can decorate these lemony delights with the simple White Icing (page 230), use a pastry bag to make swirly or stripy shape, or simply sprinkle them with some sugar.

1 cup nonhydrogenated margarine, softened
¾ cup confectioners' sugar
1½ cups all-purpose flour
1 teaspoon vanilla extract
2 tablespoons finely grated lemon zest
¼ teaspoon salt
Granulated sugar for sprinkling on the tops

In a mixing bowl beat together the margarine and confectioners' sugar until light and fluffy. Add the flour in 2 batches, beating well after each addition. Add the remaining ingredients and mix well. Mold the dough into a disk, wrap in plastic wrap, and refrigerate for at least 2 hours, until firm.

Preheat oven to 325°F; line two baking sheets with parchment paper.

Roll out dough on a lightly floured surface. Cut with 2-inch cookie cutters (heart and star shapes are awesome). Place the cookies 1 inch apart on the prepared baking sheets, sprinkle with granulated sugar, and bake for 6 to 8 minutes. Cool on the baking sheets for 2 minutes, then transfer to cooling racks to cool. Place the dough scraps in the fridge and roll them out again to make more cookies.

COOKIES AND BARS

VEGAN WITH VENGEANCE

Fig Not-ins

I wuv these cookie bar things. They are larger than your store-bought fig sandwich cookies, but bigger is better, right? They're a great snack for a brown bag lunch.

FOR THE DOUGH:
- ¼ cup nonhydrogenated margarine, softened
- ¼ cup nonhydrogenated shortening (such as Spectrum)
- ¾ cups sugar
- 2 tablespoons tapioca starch or arrowroot or cornstarch
- ¼ cup rice or soy milk
- 2 teaspoons vanilla extract
- 2 cups all-purpose flour
- ½ teaspoon baking powder
- ½ teaspoon baking soda
- ½ teaspoon salt

FOR THE FILLING:
- 1 pound dried mission figs, chopped
- ½ cup water
- ¼ cup sugar
- 1 teaspoon finely grated lemon zest

Prepare the dough:

In a mixing bowl, cream together the margarine, shortening, and sugar. Add the tapioca starch and mix well. Beat in the rice milk and vanilla. Add the flour, baking powder, baking soda, and salt, and mix well. Divide the dough into two portions, wrap in plastic wrap, and refrigerate for about an hour.

Prepare the filling:

Combine all the filling ingredients in a saucepan. Bring to a boil, then lower the heat and simmer for 5 minutes or so, stirring often. Let cool before assembling the cookies for baking.

To prepare cookies:

Preheat oven to 350°F. Lightly grease a baking sheet.

On a lightly floured surface, roll out one portion of the dough into a rectangle roughly 9 × 15 inches (you don't need to be too precise about it, it's okay if it's not

VEGAN WITH A VENGEANCE

perfectly rectangular). Divide the dough lengthwise into three equal strips. Place the three strips on baking sheet a few inches apart and divide the filling equally among the dough strips, creating a line of filling along the center with ½ inch of space on either side of the filling.

Roll out the second batch of dough to the same dimensions and cut into three strips. Place this dough over the filling-topped one and seal the edges by lightly pressing with your fingertips. Cut into 1½-inch lengths but don't separate them. Bake for about 18 minutes, until lightly browned. Let cool on baking sheet for 2 minutes, then cut each cookie again to separate and transfer to a cooling rack to cool completely.

VEGAN WITH A VENGEANCE

I've had dinner parties where I spent practically the whole time explaining the meal to my guests, with all sorts of excuses as to what went wrong. "Well you see usually the dough is more tender but I let my cat mix the batter and you all know how cats can be. . . ." One day I brought a batch of brownies to my office job and I was just done explaining to my cubicle friends why they weren't as fudgy as usual when my friend Jamie from Kentucky pulled me aside and said, "Never apologize for your food." I have taken that advice to heart and sure, if you use salt instead of sugar in your cookies then just don't serve them, but if things come out a little different from what you were expecting just go with it. Now that's Southern class.

VEGAN WITH A VENGEANCE

Chocolate Thumbprint Cookies

People love thumbprint cookies. The name and the cute little dollop of jam always elicit awwws from the masses.

1 cup all-purpose flour
1/3 cup cocoa powder
1/4 teaspoon salt
1/4 teaspoon baking soda
1/3 cup peanut oil
1/3 cup soy milk
1 teaspoon vanilla extract
1/2 teaspoon almond extract
2/3 cup sugar
6 teaspoons jam (I like raspberry or apricot)

Preheat oven to 350°F; line two cookie sheets with parchment paper.

Sift together the flour, cocoa powder, salt, and baking soda.

In a large bowl mix together all the wet ingredients (except the jam) plus the sugar. Add the dry ingredients to the wet and incorporate well.

With damp hands, roll 1 tablespoon of dough into a ball and press between your palms into a disk, then place on a prepared cookie sheet. It's important to the texture of the cookies that your hands are damp, to prevent cracking at the edges. Bake the cookies for 5 minutes, then remove from oven. Press your thumb into each cookie to make an indent. They're pretty hot at this point so proceed carefully, or use something thumblike to make the indent. Place 1/4 teaspoon of jam into each indentation. Bake another 6 minutes. Remove from oven and let sit for two minutes, then transfer to a cooling rack to cool.

COOKIES AND BARS

VEGAN WITH A
VENGEANCE

Banana Split Pudding Brownies

This is a really fudgy brownie with a banana pudding on top that melts into the brownie layer and forms this unbelievable ooey gooey banana brownie concoction. Although you can hold it in your hand, you may want to serve it with a fork.

FOR THE BROWNIES:
> 4 ounces semisweet chocolate, chopped
> 1 cup mashed very ripe banana (about 2 large bananas)
> ⅓ cup canola oil
> 1 cup sugar
> 1 teaspoon vanilla extract
> ¾ cup all-purpose flour
> ¼ cup cocoa powder
> ¼ teaspoon baking soda
> ⅛ teaspoon salt

FOR THE TOPPING LAYER:
> 1 cup mashed very ripe banana
> 2 tablespoons sugar
> ¼ cup soy milk
> ½ teaspoon vanilla extract
> 1 tablespoon arrowroot powder

FOR DECORATION AND MORE BANANA YUMMINESS:
> 1 ripe but not very ripe banana, thinly sliced

Preheat oven to 350°F. Spray a 9 × 13-inch baking pan with nonstick cooking spray or very lightly grease with oil.

To make the brownie batter:

Melt the chocolate by placing in a pan or heat-proof mixing bowl over a small pot of boiling water. Stir with a heatproof spatula until completely melted, then remove from heat and set aside to cool.

In a large mixing bowl, combine 1 cup of mashed banana, the oil, and the sugar. Use a handheld mixer to beat everything together for about a minute. If you don't have a mixer, use a strong fork and mix for about 3 minutes. Mix in the vanilla and the melted chocolate.

In a separate bowl, sift together the flour, cocoa powder, baking soda, and salt. Add this to the banana mixture in batches, mixing with the hand mixer as you go along. Mix for about 1 minute more.

Prepare the banana topping:

In a small bowl, combine all topping ingredients and mix with the hand mixer (remember to rinse the beaters off first) for about a minute.

To assemble and bake the brownies:

Spread the brownie batter evenly into baking pan. Pour the banana topping over that and spread evenly. Bake for 30 minutes. Remove from oven and let cool. After about 15 minutes, move it to the fridge until fully cooled. Cut into twelve squares, place a few slices of banana on top of each portion, and serve.

VEGAN WITH
VENGEANCE

Macadamia Blondies with Caramel-Maple Topping

Macadamias make these blondies rich and buttery. They are great unfrosted if you don't want something too sweet but the caramel-maple topping makes for a decadent treat.

FOR THE BLONDIES:
2¾ cups all-purpose flour
1 teaspoon baking powder
1 teaspoon baking soda
½ teaspoon salt
6 ounces firm silken tofu (this is half a package of the vacuum-packed kind)
¼ cup rice or soy milk
⅓ cup canola oil
2 cups sugar
2 tablespoons vanilla extract
1¼ cups raw macadamias, partially chopped and partially ground (see Punk Points on next page)

FOR THE TOPPING:
¼ cup nonhydrogenated margarine
2 tablespoons turbinado or other brown sugar
¼ cup pure maple syrup
1 cup raw macadamia nuts, coarsely chopped

Preheat oven to 350°F. Lightly grease a 9 × 13-inch baking pan.

To prepare the dough:

In a large bowl, sift together the flour, baking powder, baking soda, and salt.

In a blender, whiz the tofu with the rice milk until smooth. Add the oil, sugar, and vanilla, and blend again. Pour the tofu mixture into the flour mixture and use a firm wooden spoon to combine everything well. Fold in the macadamias. The batter will be thick and have a cookie dough consistency. Spread in the baking pan and bake for 25 minutes. Meanwhile, prepare the topping.

VEGAN WITH A VENGEANCE

To prepare the topping:

In a saucepan over medium heat, combine the margarine, turbinado sugar, and maple syrup, and heat until the sugar dissolves. Increase the heat to bring to a boil for 1 minute. Stir in the nuts. Remove from heat.

Remove the blondies from oven and pour the topping over them, return to oven, and bake for 10 more minutes.

Let cool completely before serving, the topping should harden to a caramel-like consistency. I cut these into sixteen squares but they are also cute as triangles.

PUNK POiNTS

The macadamias should be partially ground and partially chopped, which is easily achieved in a food processor with about 30 pulses. If you don't have a food processor then chop all the macadamias, put half of them aside, and continue to chop the others or grind them in a blender until they resemble coarse crumbs.

VEGAN WITH A VENGEANCE

Raspberry–Chocolate Chip Blondie Bars

These are blondies topped with a raspberry spread and chocolate chips, then finished off with some of the blondie batter dropped on top. They're tantalizing and cool looking and kids seem to really enjoy them. If you are low on time you can use 1 cup of raspberry preserves or raspberry jam in place of the raspberry layer.

FOR RASPBERRY LAYER:

2 cups frozen raspberries

3 tablespoons tapioca starch (you can substitute arrowroot or cornstarch)

¼ cup cold water

⅓ cup sugar

FOR THE BLONDIE LAYER:

3¾ cups all-purpose flour

1¼ teaspoons baking soda

½ teaspoon salt

1 (6-ounce) container plain or vanilla soy yogurt

¼ cup rice milk

½ cup plus 2 tablespoons canola oil

2 cups sugar

1 tablespoon vanilla extract

1 cup chocolate chips

Preheat oven to 350°F. Lightly grease a 9 × 13-inch baking pan.

Prepare the raspberry layer:

In a saucepan combine all raspberry layer ingredients and stir until the tapioca starch is dissolved. Bring to a boil and then lower to a low boil, stirring often, for 5 minutes or until thickened. Remove from heat.

Prepare the blondie layer:

In a mixing bowl sift together the flour, baking soda, and salt. In a separate bowl, combine the soy yogurt, rice milk, oil, sugar, and vanilla. In batches, mix the dry ingredients into the wet to form a dough. Set aside 1 cup of the dough and spread the rest in the prepared baking pan. Spread the raspberry layer over it (or use 1 cup of raspberry preserves). Sprinkle half of the chocolate chips over the raspberry layer. Drop the remaining dough over the chips and raspberries; sprinkle the rest of the chocolate chips over that. Bake for 35 minutes. Let cool completely before serving.

VEGAN WITH A VENGEANCE

Date-Nut Diamonds

Okay, you don't have to cut these into diamonds, but they look cute if you choose to. These bars are very Home and Garden.

> 1 cup all-purpose flour
> ⅛ teaspoon salt
> ½ cup nonhydrogenated margarine
> ¾ cup dried dates, roughly chopped
> ¾ cup brown sugar
> 1 cup chopped walnuts
> ½ cup unsweetened shredded coconut
> 1 teaspoon vanilla extract
> 2 tablespoons tapioca starch

Preheat oven to 375°F. Lightly grease an 11×17-inch baking pan.

In a medium-size bowl combine the flour and the salt. Cut in the margarine using a pastry knife or your fingers until you've got coarse crumbs. Press the mixture into the bottom of the prepared pan. Bake for 12 minutes.

In a small saucepan place the dates in enough water to cover. Bring to a boil; reduce heat, cover, and simmer for 10 minutes; drain.

In a mixing bowl stir together the cooked dates, brown sugar, walnuts, coconut, and vanilla. Sprinkle with the tapioca starch and stir till combined. Spread evenly over the partially baked crust. Bake for 15 minutes. Remove from oven and let cool. Cut into diamonds by cutting strips lengthwise, then diagonally.

VEGAN WITH A VENGEANCE

Finally, dessert! The most common cooking-type complaint I hear from people is that they can't bake. I don't know what the problem is but wouldn't it be worth it to learn so that you can have cakes and cupcakes and pies? Get an oven thermometer, a timer, and appropriate pans and I assure you, you can bake! This chapter is definitely my baby and the one I found myself testing the recipes for over and over and over again. Enjoy!

DESSERTS

The election of 2004 was hard on everyone. The day John Kerry lost I went to Prospect Park and sat in the middle of the field. I took comfort in the feeling of the grass and dirt below me as I sat alone in the empty meadow and I was a bit scared to leave because I thought that in my liberal neighborhood there would be panic on the streets.

Months later people were still analyzing why he lost. Was it fear? Was it homophobia? Was it bible-thumping? I thought back to what the lefties did "wrong" and the only thing that I could really put my finger on was this one "Baking against Bush" bake sale I went to. There were actually store-bought items, wrapped in plastic. Good people, that is not a bake sale. I am sure that in Texas, if they were to hold a "Baking for Bush" bake sale, there would be no factory-baked cupcakes. In fact, I am sure something like that would rank right up there with gay marriage. If we as a movement want to succeed, our bake sales must reflect that. We must have fresh-baked cookies, cupcakes loaded with icing. We must take the time to pipe those gingerbread decorations with all our might. Otherwise we are in the business of reselling capitalism. Our bake sales must come from our hearts and our ovens (at the correct temperatures) in order for us to be taken seriously. In this chapter I've included some items that will help usher in the revolution.

Ginger-Macadamia-Coconut-Carrot Cake

If I were to make a commercial for this carrot cake it would feature a family in middle America going, "What's for dessert?" and then the mom, with perfectly coifed hair and dishtowels in her hands says, "Carrot cake," and then the kids with bowl haircuts say, "Carrot cake again?" and put their face in their hands. The husband puffs on his pipe and buries his face in the newspaper, completely uninterested. But the mom's got a mischievous look in her eye; she brings out the carrot cake and suddenly there is a calypso band in the dining room and the kids start dancing, heck even grandma joins in the dance. What I am saying is that this is not your average carrot cake. Feel free to replace the macadamia nuts with their more affordable cousins, walnuts.

2⅓ cups all-purpose flour
1 tablespoon baking powder
1 teaspoon baking soda
¾ teaspoon salt
2 teaspoons ground cinnamon
½ teaspoon ground or freshly grated nutmeg
1 cup pineapple juice
½ cup canola oil
¾ cup sugar
½ cup pure maple syrup
2 teaspoons vanilla extract
1 cup macadamia nuts, roughly chopped
¼ cup crystallized ginger, chopped (even better if you can find small pieces specifically for baking)
1 cup unsweetened shredded coconut
2 cups carrots, grated

Preheat oven to 350°F. Have ready two 8-inch round springform cake pans, lightly greased. Alternatively, this could be made in a 9 × 13-inch baking pan and cut in half lengthwise to create two layers or just iced as one layer.

In a large mixing bowl sift together the flour, baking powder, baking soda, salt, and ground spices.

In a separate large mixing bowl, mix together the pineapple, oil, sugar, maple syrup, and vanilla. Add the dry ingredients to the wet in batches, and combine well with a hand mixer or strong fork. Fold in the macadamias, ginger, coconut, and carrots.

Divide the batter evenly between the two round cake pans, or spread in the rectangular pan, and bake for 40 to 45 minutes. Let cool in pans. Remove from pans and put a layer of coconut icing (page 227) between the layers, and another layer of coconut icing on top; I like to leave the sides free of frosting because it looks pretty.

VEGAN WITH A VENGEANCE

Raspberry Blackout Cake with Ganache-y Frosting

This makes a great birthday cake and I have found that even people who think that they aren't crazy about chocolate and raspberries go crazy over it. The recipe calls for a lot of frosting (recipe follows) because I'm hoping that you will get some cake decorating bags and have some fun decorating the top with chocolate roses. If I am wrong and you absolutely will not, then you can get away with halving the frosting recipe.

> 1½ cups all-purpose flour
> ½ cup Dutch-processed cocoa powder
> 1 teaspoon baking powder
> 1 teaspoon baking soda
> ½ teaspoon salt
> 1½ cups plain rice or soy milk
> ½ cup canola oil
> 1 (10-ounce) jar raspberry preserves (reserve ½ cup for the batter)
> 2 teaspoons vanilla extract
> 1¼ cups sugar
> Fresh raspberries for decorating and yumminess

Preheat oven to 350°F. Spray two 8-inch round springform cake pans with cooking spray. If you don't have springform then use parchment paper rounds on the bottom of two ordinary 8-inch round cake pans to prevent sticking.

Sift together the flour, cocoa powder, baking powder, baking soda, and salt. Combine the rice milk, oil, ½ cup of the preserves, the vanilla, and the sugar in a large bowl and mix with a hand mixer or strong fork. The jam should be mostly dissolved with the rest of the ingredients; some small clumps are okay. Add the dry ingredients to the wet in batches and mix until everything is incorporated. Divide the batter between the prepared pans and bake at 350°F for 40 to 45 minutes, or until a toothpick or knife comes out clean. Remove from oven and let cool in pans.

When the cakes have cooled fully, spread one layer of cake with a thin layer of the reserved raspberry preserves (give the preserves a quick mix with a strong fork to get a spreadable consistency); spread a layer of chocolate frosting on top of the preserves. Place the other layer of cake on top and spread its top with preserves. Carefully spread the chocolate frosting over the top, then ice the sides. I like to put

VEGAN WITH A
VENGEANCE

a circle of fresh raspberries around the circumference of the top. If you happen to have a decorating bag and tips around, you can alternate a rosebud or star flourish with a raspberry, and a few raspberries in the center will finish it off.

Chocolate Ganache-y Frosting

¾ cup soy creamer (I use Silk Soy Creamer but if it's not available plain soy milk will do)
6 tablespoons nonhydrogenated margarine
10 ounces semisweet chocolate chips

In a saucepan over medium heat, bring the soy creamer to a low boil. Add the margarine and melt, turn off the heat, and stir in chocolate chips until smooth. Let sit for at least 1 hour. It should still have a pourable consistency at this point. If you want a spreadable consistency then refrigerate for an hour. (If you refrigerate it for more than a few hours, it sets too much to spread easily, so you will need to reheat it, then let it sit at room temperature before using.)

VEGAN WITH A VENGEANCE

Orange-Rum Tea Cake

This is a nice intensely orange cake perfect as an afternoon cake whilst you take tea with your other white-gloved socialite friends. There's no frosting, just a simple orange rum syrup that takes all of three minutes to put together, and it forms a nice caramelly base for the slivered almonds. If you don't have a 9-inch springform pan, a brownie pan, or a smaller round pan works well; just increase the baking time by about 10 minutes and use parchment paper to prevent sticking. You will need about six Valencia-size oranges to get the amount of juice needed.

FOR THE CAKE:

1 (6-ounce) container soy yogurt

⅓ cup oil

¾ cup sugar

¼ cup soy milk

¼ cup freshly squeezed orange juice

4 teaspoons finely grated fresh orange zest

1 teaspoon vanilla extract

1¼ cups all-purpose flour

¼ cup yellow cornmeal

1½ teaspoons baking powder

½ teaspoon salt

½ cup slivered almonds

FOR ORANGE RUM SYRUP:

⅓ cup freshly squeezed orange juice

2 tablespoons sugar

2 tablespoons rum

Preheat oven to 350°F. Spray your cake pan with nonstick cooking spray or lightly grease with oil.

In a large bowl, mix together the soy yogurt, oil, and sugar. Add the soy milk, orange juice, orange zest, and vanilla. Mix well to combine.

I like to sift the dry ingredients directly into the wet at this point, but you can also use a separate bowl to sift together the flour, cornmeal, baking powder, and salt, and then add that to the wet mixture, and mix to combine.

Transfer the batter to the prepared baking pan and bake until golden, when a toothpick or knife inserted in center comes out clean, about 35 minutes.

VEGAN WITH VENGEANCE

Remove from oven and let cool 10 minutes or until you can handle the pan and remove the cake; let it cool upside down or on a cooling rack. At this point you should prepare the syrup.

In a small saucepan, bring the orange juice and sugar to a boil over medium-high heat, stirring constantly until the sugar is dissolved. Lower the heat to a simmer, add the rum, and simmer for 2 more minutes. Remove from heat and let cool completely.

When the cake has cooled completely, place on a serving plate and arrange the slivered almonds on top. Pour the cooled orange syrup over the top; let sit for a couple of minutes to absorb the syrup. Serve.

Chocolate-Rum Pudding Cake

SERVES 8–10

I found a recipe like this in a cookbook for one-bowl desserts and decided to veganize it. The rum flavor isn't overpowering at all, it just adds a little hint of sumthin' sumthin'. You can serve it warm with the pudding layer oozing all over the place, or serve it chilled with the pudding layer nice and thick on the top. It's a quick recipe that will make people think it took more work than it really did. If you are a pathological liar, just go ahead and let them think that.

1 cup all-purpose flour
2 teaspoons baking powder
½ teaspoon baking soda
¼ teaspoon salt
1 cup sugar
½ cup Dutch-processed cocoa powder
½ cup plain soy milk
¼ cup canola oil
1 teaspoon vanilla extract
1 teaspoon rum extract (or just use 1 more teaspoon vanilla if you don't have rum extract)
½ cup pure maple syrup
¼ cup light rum
½ cup boiling water

Boil some water in a teakettle, preheat oven to 350°F, and grease a 9-inch round springform cake pan.

Sift together the flour, baking powder, baking soda, salt, ¾ cup of the sugar, and ¼ cup of the cocoa powder. Add the soy milk, oil, and extracts, and mix into a thick batter. Spread the batter in the prepared cake pan. Sprinkle the top with the remaining cocoa powder and sugar. Pour ½ cup of boiling water into a glass measuring cup, add the maple syrup and rum to the water, and pour this mixture on top of the cake batter.

Place the cake on a cookie sheet in case of pudding overflow and bake for 30 to 35 minutes. Let cool just a bit; while it's still warm, place the cake on a large plate and release the sides (your plate should have a slight rim to prevent spillage). Throw on a scoop of vanilla soy ice cream if you like and you've got yourself one impressive dessert.

221

DESSERTS

VEGAN WITH A VENGEANCE

I'm a chubby girl. I say it proudly and with no bad feelings. I'm happy with my body (except for those days when I hate it) but sometimes my weight pushes past my comfort zone (writing cookbooks doesn't help this) and I need to lose a few pounds. Losing weight doesn't mean I have to stop eating cookies and cupcakes, it just means I have to change how I prepare them and then somehow get myself to consume only one. So if you, too, occasionally bust out of your bullet belt, here are some tips for healthier baking.

Making your baked foods low fat is really super-duper easy. I'm almost ashamed to write about it because it's such a gimme. There are two fat substitutes that I use: pureed prunes or applesauce. The great thing about these fat replacers is that they also work as binding agents (meaning they help hold the cake together), so it's a win-win situation. Generally, I use the prunes in chocolate things and the applesauce in anything that isn't chocolate. The applesauce doesn't usually leave any sort of a taste but the prunes give a somewhat "healthy" (for lack of a better word) taste to things, but it adds a nice dimension to chocolate things. Don't be afraid to convert any of the baked goods in this book; I have made them all low fat at one point or another and I know that it will work.

For prunes, if the recipe calls for ½ cup of oil or margarine, then fill a liquid measuring cup to about the ⅓ cup mark. I wouldn't advise using any more than that because it may make the finished product too moist. Hold the prunes down with your hand so that they don't float up, and add the apple juice or water or whatever liquid you might be using in the recipe (soy or rice milk, for instance). Then transfer to a blender and puree until very smooth. For applesauce, follow the same guideline. Use ⅓ cup of applesauce in place of ½ cup of oil or margarine. Expect the finished product to be cakier than usual. Whether I choose prunes or applesauce I always add 2 teaspoons of oil to the recipe at the point when the liquids are combined with the dry ingredients. It's a small amount but goes a long way to improving the texture. I also remove 2 tablespoons of sugar for every ½ cup of prune puree used.

Fiber is also an important factor in weight loss. White flour has very little fiber, and you lose a lot of the nutrients from the original grain. Regular whole wheat flour, however, will give things a grainy texture and too strong a wheaty taste. I like to use whole-wheat pastry flour instead; it's all the bran and germ of whole wheat but ground to a soft, fine flour; it will work wonderfully in all your sweet baked treats. Use it in place of all-purpose flour. I often use half whole-wheat pastry flour and half all-purpose flour.

So go ahead and have that cookie, and if you are scared you will eat all of them in the middle of the night just send them my way.

Blueberry Coffee Cake

In my country, coffee cake doesn't actually have any coffee in it, it's just a cake that goes well with coffee. I had to quit coffee anyway, so I eat my cake with tea, although in my heart of hearts I know it's a coffee cake. This is the perfect treat if you want to get warm fuzzies inside.

FOR THE TOPPING:
- ¼ cup all-purpose flour
- 3 tablespoons brown sugar
- ¼ teaspoon ground cinnamon
- 1 tablespoon canola oil
- 1 cup chopped walnuts

FOR THE CAKE:
- 4 cups all-purpose flour
- 1 tablespoon baking powder
- 1 teaspoon baking soda
- 1½ teaspoons salt
- 1½ teaspoons ground cinnamon
- ¼ teaspoon ground allspice
- ¼ cup canola oil
- 1 (6-ounce) container vanilla soy yogurt
- 1 cup pure maple syrup
- 1½ cups plain soy milk
- 1 teaspoon vanilla extract
- 2 cups fresh blueberries

Preheat oven to 350°F. Lightly grease or spray a 9 × 13-inch baking pan with nonstick cooking spray.

Make the topping:
Sift together the flour, brown sugar, and cinnamon. Drizzle in the oil a little at a time and mix with your fingertips until crumbs form. Add the walnuts and mix.

Make the cake:
Sift together the dry ingredients into a large bowl. In a separate bowl, vigorously whisk together the wet ingredients until well combined. Add the wet ingredients to the dry and mix well. Fold in the blueberries.

VEGAN WITH A VENGEANCE

Spread the batter in the prepared pan and sprinkle the topping over it. Bake for 45 minutes, or until a toothpick or knife comes out clean. Tastes great still warm.

PUNK POINTS

You can substitute frozen blueberries for fresh but keep them in the freezer till the last possible moment to prevent thawing that might turn the batter purple.

VEGAN WITH VENGEANCE

*T*his is an interview I did for the cupcakelicious blog—Cupcakes Take the Cake (www.cupcakestakethecake.blogspot.com/)

Name: Isa Chandra Moskowitz
Age: 32
Location: Prospect Heights, Brooklyn
Occupation: Wage slave and Celebrity Chef of the People
Web site: www.theppk.com

How often do you eat cupcakes? At least once a week

What's the best thing about eating cupcakes? They say that the first thing you eat with is your eyes, and I really like to look at my cupcake first. I think most other people do, too. When you hand someone a slice of cake, sure, they're happy, but hand them a cupcake and they are dazzled. They spin it around and look at it from every angle.

What's your favorite type of cupcake? I've been on a citrus kick lately, but it's just a phase. I like a devil's food cupcake with ganache icing.

Favorite place to get cupcakes? Well veganism makes cupcake procurement a mite difficult. Veg City Diner used to have them but they've gone out of business. I usually make them myself so my answer would have to be "in my kitchen."

How do cupcakes compare/contrast to other baked goods for you? If there's a cupcake option I would choose that above all others. Cupcake eating is more of an experience or an activity. With other baked goods you're just having dessert.

Is there any innovation you'd like to see made to the cupcake that would improve it for you? I would like to see more self-filling cupcake recipes. That is, cupcakes with the filling baked right inside rather than piping it in. I'm working on it.

Any other thoughts on the topic? My childhood cat was named Cupcake, she went to kitty heaven in 2000. I tip a metaphorical 40 to her memory every time I eat a cupcake.

Coconut Heaven Cupcakes

These are a must for the coconut lovers in your life: dense coconut cupcakes topped off with fluffy coconut icing to die for, thus the name Coconut Heaven Cupcakes.

FOR THE CUPCAKES:

1 cup all-purpose flour
½ teaspoon baking powder
½ teaspoon baking soda
¼ teaspoon salt
¼ cup canola oil
1 cup coconut milk
⅔ cup sugar
1 teaspoon vanilla extract
1 cup unsweetened shredded coconut

FOR THE FROSTING:

¼ cup nonhydrogenated margarine at room temperature
¼ cup coconut milk
1 teaspoon vanilla extract
2 cups confectioners' sugar, sifted
1 cup unsweetened coconut

Bake the cupcakes:

Preheat oven to 350°F. Line a twelve-muffin tin with paper liners, set aside.

Sift together the flour, baking powder, baking soda, and salt. In a separate bowl combine the oil, coconut milk, sugar, and vanilla. Pour the dry ingredients into the wet and mix until smooth. Fold in 1 cup unsweetened coconut. Use an ice-cream scoop to fill each muffin tin about two-thirds full. Bake at 350°F for 20 to 22 minutes; the cupcakes should be slightly browned around the edges and spring back when touched. Remove them from the muffin tin and place on a cooling rack.

Make the frosting:

Cream the margarine until light and fluffy. Add the coconut milk and vanilla and combine. Add the sifted confectioners' sugar and mix until smooth (use an electric handheld mixer; otherwise it might take a good 5 minutes to mix). Add the unsweetened coconut and combine. Refrigerate until ready to use.

Frost when the cupcakes have cooled fully. You can sprinkle a little more unsweetened coconut on top if you like, or put a berry on them for a little color.

VEGAN WITH A VENGEANCE

Lemon Gem Cupcakes

These are sophisticated cupcakes. They don't peek over the wrapper; the icing comes right to the top. Once baked the cupcake gives off an iridescent glow, but don't worry, you are not living in a postapocalyptic world of glowing food, it's just the abundance of the lemon.

> 1⅓ cups all-purpose flour
> ½ teaspoon baking powder
> ¾ teaspoon baking soda
> ¼ teaspoon salt
> ¼ cup canola oil
> ⅔ cup plus 2 tablespoons sugar
> 1 cup rice milk
> 1 teaspoon vanilla extract
> ¼ cup lemon juice
> 1 tablespoon lemon zest

Preheat oven to 350°F. Line a twelve-muffin tin with paper liners.

Sift together the flour, baking powder, baking soda, and salt. In a separate bowl combine the oil, sugar, rice milk, vanilla, lemon juice, and lemon zest. Pour the dry ingredients into the wet and mix until smooth. Fill each muffin cup about two-thirds full; bake for 17 to 20 minutes. Remove the cupcakes from muffin tin and place on a cooling rack. Frost when cooled fully.

Lemon Frosting

> ¼ cup nonhydrogenated soy margarine, softened
> ¼ cup soy milk
> 2 tablespoons lemon juice
> 2 cups confectioners' sugar, sifted

Whisk the margarine with a fork until fluffy. Stir in the soy milk and lemon juice; add the confectioners' sugar and mix until smooth. (It may take 5 minutes or so to get it to be the right consistency unless you employ an electric handheld mixer). Refrigerate until ready to use.

VEGAN WITH A VENGEANCE

Fauxstess Cupcakes

If I could only eat one cupcake for the rest of my life, well, first I would wonder what I did to deserve such punishment, and then I would choose these. And I think I know someone that would agree with me—the entire country of America. These are my take on those cream-filled chocolate cupcakes with the swirls on top whose name shall not be mentioned. They take a long time, there are many steps, but they are so worth it. Black cocoa powder is hard to find, but you need it to get the exact right flavor and color. If you can't find it, you can sub Dutch-processed cocoa, or don't sweat it, the cupcakes are still damn good. Don't skip the sifting step; the cocoa tends to clump up, and no one likes clumps. The recipe doubles really well, so go ahead and make a double batch.

1 cup unbleached all-purpose flour
¼ cup cocoa powder
3 tablespoons black cocoa powder
1 teaspoon baking powder
½ teaspoon baking soda
¼ teaspoon salt
1 cup plain rice or soy milk
¼ cup canola oil
½ cup pure maple syrup
¼ cup sugar
1 teaspoon apple cider vinegar
1 teaspoon vanilla extract

Preheat oven to 350°F. Line a twelve-muffin tin with paper liners, spray the liners with canola cooking spray.

In a medium-size mixing bowl, sift together the flour, cocoa powders, baking powder, baking soda, and salt. In a large mixing bowl combine the rice milk, oil, maple syrup, sugar, vinegar, and vanilla, and beat at medium speed with an electric handheld mixer for a good 2 minutes. Add the dry ingredients to the wet in two batches, mixing as you go. Beat for about a minute more.

Use a wet ice-cream scoop to fill the cupcake liner three-quarters full. Bake for about 28 minutes, until a toothpick inserted in the center comes out clean. Transfer to a cooling rack. Time to make the Fluffy White Icing.

VEGAN WITH A
VENGEANCE

Fluffy White icing

¼ cup nonhydrogenated margarine
½ cup nonhydrogenated shortening
¾ cup superfine (or caster) sugar
¼ cup plain soy milk powder (don't use low-fat, it has a "taste")
2 teaspoons vanilla extract (get the highest quality you can; the kind that's thick
    and syrupy tastes best)
Pinch salt

In a medium-size mixing bowl, beat together the margarine and shortening with an electric handheld mixer on medium speed until well combined. Add the sugar and soy milk powder and beat for a good 10 minutes until very fluffy. Add vanilla extract and a pinch of salt, and beat for another minute. You may want to do a little taste test and add a little more sugar if needed. On to the Ganache:

Chocolate Ganache icing

⅓ cup soy milk
4 ounces bittersweet chocolate, chopped
2 tablespoons pure maple syrup

In a small saucepan, scorch the soy milk (bring it to a boil), then lower the heat to a simmer and add the chocolate and maple syrup. Mix with a heatproof spatula for about 30 seconds. Turn the heat off, and continue stirring until the chocolate is fully melted and the icing is smooth. Next, make the icing for the squigglies:

Royal icing for the Squigglies

2 cups confectioners' sugar
2 tablespoons soy milk powder
2 tablespoons water

Sift the sugar into a mixing bowl. Add the soy milk powder. Add 1 tablespoon of the water and stir, then add the rest of the water a little bit at a time until you reach a consistency slightly more solid than toothpaste. The icing should not be drippy at all; if it is add a little more confectioners' sugar.

Assemble the cupcakes:

You will need two cake decorators' bags, one fitted with a small round tip (the kind you use for writing) and one fitted with a large star-shaped or round tip.

Fill the large-tipped one with Fluffy White Icing; fill the writing one with Royal Icing.

Poke a hole in the center of each cupcake, using your pinkie. Cram the tip of the bag with the Fluffy White Icing into the hole and squeeze to get as much icing into the center as you can, slowly drawing out the bag, until the icing fills to the top of the hole.

Wipe the excess icing off the top of the cupcake with a napkin or (if you're me) your finger.

Dip the top of each cupcake into the Chocolate Ganache Icing. Tilt the pan to add more depth to the icing for easier cupcake coating. Place all the cupcakes on a cutting board, make some room in your fridge, and put the cupcakes in there to set the ganache, about 10 minutes.

Use these 10 minutes to practice your squigglies for the tops. I use my left hand to steady my writing hand by holding onto my right wrist. Practice a bit and see what works for you.

Remove the cupcakes from the fridge and make your squiggles on the top of the ganache. Return to the fridge to set. I like to keep the cupcakes in there till I'm ready to serve them.

VEGAN WITH A VENGEANCE

No-Bake Black Bottom–Peanut Butter Silk Pie

SERVES 8

Peanut butter and chocolate. Need I say more? Okay, this is rich, creamy, and what's more is you don't have to bake it. I listed the milks to use in order of preference; I have made it with all four and I like coconut milk the best, but it's good with the others as well.

1 prepared Chocolate Cookie Pie Crust (recipe follows) or graham cracker crust

FOR CHOCOLATE BOTTOM:
- **4 ounces semisweet chocolate**
- **¼ cup rice or soy milk**

FOR THE FILLING:
- **12 ounces extra-firm silken tofu (the vacuum-packed kind, like Mori-Nu)**
- **¾ cup creamy all-natural peanut butter**
- **1½ cups confectioners' sugar**
- **2 teaspoons vanilla extract**
- **⅔ cup coconut milk, soy creamer, rice milk, or soy milk**
- **1¼ cups boiling water**
- **3 tablespoons agar**

Prepare the black bottom:

Melt the chocolate in a makeshift double boiler (page 206). When the chocolate has melted, add the soy milk and whisk until smooth. Remove from heat. Pour most of this mixture into the prepared pie crust, reserving a couple of tablespoons to drizzle over the top of the pie. Transfer the chocolate-coated pie crust to the fridge.

Make the filling:

Combine the tofu, peanut butter, sugar, and vanilla in a blender or food processor. Blend until smooth.

In a saucepan over moderate heat, boil the agar in 1¼ cups boiling water. Stir constantly until dissolved. This takes about 10 minutes. When dissolved, pour into a glass measuring cup (if you have only plastic, let the mixture cool just a bit before pouring it into the cup, so it doesn't melt the plastic).

232 | DESSERTS

There is usually ⅓ cup agar at this point. You want the liquids to be 1 cup but you can't add it to the agar mixture or it will firm up, so if you have ⅓ cup agar and water, add ⅔ cup of milk to the tofu mixture and blend. Then add the agar and blend again.

Assemble the pie:

Slowly pour the peanut butter mixture into the pie crust. Drizzle the remaining chocolate over the pie. Run a butter knife through the chocolate in straight lines to create a pretty pattern. Refrigerate, wrapped in plastic wrap, for at least 3 hours.

No-Bake Chocolate Cookie Pie Crust

You can use any chocolate cookie that is waferlike. I like to use Newman's Tops and Bottoms, but if those are not available, try Nature's Path Deep Chocolate cookies.

> 1½ cups chocolate cookies, crushed
> 2 tablespoons sugar
> ⅛ teaspoon salt
> ¼ cup canola oil
> 1 tablespoon rice or soy milk

In a food processor fitted with a steel blade, or a blender, combine the cookies, sugar, and salt. Pulse into fine crumbs. Remove from the processor and pour into a pie plate. Drizzle with the canola oil and mix with your fingers. Drizzle with the soy milk and mix with your fingers. Press into the pie plate. Refrigerate until ready to use.

VEGAN WITH A
VENGEANCE

Sweet Potato Pie with Three-Nut Topping

This is one of the first recipes I ever got off the Internet and veganized, so it is close to my heart. I love the combination of the three nuts but you can improvise with just one nut of your choosing; pecans are a great choice. Some people think sweet potatoes should only be a side dish and not a dessert; those people are not to be trusted so keep your distance.

FOR THE GRAHAM CRACKER CRUST:
⅓ cup walnuts, toasted
⅓ cup hazelnuts, toasted
⅓ cup almonds, toasted
10 graham cracker sheets
¼ cup firmly packed dark brown sugar
Pinch each of ground ginger, nutmeg, cinnamon, and allspice
5 tablespoons canola oil

FOR THE FILLING:
1¼ pounds sweet potatoes
2 tablespoons arrowroot
½ cup sugar
½ cup soy milk
3 tablespoons canola oil
2 tablespoons pure maple syrup
6 ounces firm silken tofu (half a package of the vacuum-packed kind)
1 teaspoon ground ginger
½ teaspoon ground nutmeg
½ teaspoon ground cinnamon
¼ teaspoon ground allspice
⅛ teaspoon ground cloves

FOR THE TOPPING:
¼ cup nonhydrogenated margarine
¼ cup brown sugar
2 tablespoons maple syrup
⅓ cup whole almonds, toasted

VEGAN WITH A VENGEANCE

⅓ cup whole hazelnuts, toasted
⅓ cup walnuts, toasted

Preheat oven to 350°F. Bake the sweet potatoes until tender, about 1 hour. Meanwhile, make the crust.

Make the crust:

Grind the nuts in a food processor, crumble in the graham crackers, and grind into crumbs. Add the sugar and spices, pulse to combine. Add the oil and pulse to moisten the crumbs. Press into a 9-inch (preferably glass) pie plate, set aside.

Make the filling:

When the sweet potatoes are done, remove them from the oven and let them cool. Puree in a food processor or blender. Add all other filling ingredients and puree until smooth. Pour the filling into the crust. Bake at 350°F until the center moves only slightly when pan is shaken, covering with foil if crust browns too quickly, about 40 minutes.

While the pie bakes, prepare the topping:

Make the topping:

Stir the margarine, sugar, and maple syrup in heavy medium-size saucepan over low heat until the sugar dissolves. Increase the heat and boil for 1 minute. Mix in the nuts, coating them completely.

Spoon the hot nut mixture over the pie. Continue baking until the topping bubbles, about 5 minutes. Transfer to a cooling rack and cool completely.

VEGAN WITH A VENGEANCE

Gingerbread Apple Pie

SERVES 8–12

I invented this one Thanksgiving when I couldn't choose between baking an apple pie or gingerbread, and it's been a holiday tradition ever since, even if I don't go to a family gathering and it's just my husband, me, and my cats. Truth be told, I hate rolling out pie crust so the crumb topping and pressed crust is a sweet relief for me. As my sister and I say, "This is jood." (We think pronouncing all g's as j's is funny; try it, you'll see.)

FOR THE CRUST:
  1½ cups all-purpose unbleached flour
  ½ cup brown sugar
  1 teaspoon ground ginger
  1 teaspoon ground cinnamon
  ¼ teaspoon ground allspice
  ½ teaspoon salt
  1 teaspoon baking powder
  ½ cup nonhydrogenated margarine, softened
  1 tablespoon molasses
  2 tablespoons cold water

FOR THE FILLING:
  2 pounds Granny Smith apples (about 8), peeled, cored, and thinly sliced
  ½ cup brown sugar
  1 teaspoon ground cinnamon
  ¼ teaspoon ground or freshly grated nutmeg
  ¼ teaspoon ground allspice
  ½ teaspoon ground ginger
  Pinch ground cloves
  ¼ cup pure maple syrup
  1 tablespoon canola oil
  2 tablespoons tapioca starch or arrowroot

Preheat oven to 375°F.

Make the crust:
  Sift together the flour, sugar, spices, salt, and baking powder. Add the margarine one tablespoonful at a time and cut in with a pastry cutter, knife, or your

236

DESSERTS

fingertips. Drizzle the molasses and water over the dough, mixing with your fingertips until the crumbs of dough begin to cling together. Set aside ½ cup of the dough. Gather together the rest of the dough and knead it into a ball. Press it evenly into the bottom and sides of a pie pan and bake for 10 minutes.

Make the filling:

While the crust bakes, combine in a mixing bowl all the filling ingredients except the tapioca starch. Sprinkle the tapioca over the apple mixture and mix until the starch is dissolved.

Assemble the pie:

Fill the pie crust with the apple mixture, and crumble the remaining ½ cup of dough over the filling. Cover with foil and bake for 20 more minutes. Remove the foil and bake 30 minutes more; the filling should be bubbling and the apples should be tender. Serve warm or at room temperature.

PUNK POINTS

Apple corers can be a pain in the butt, so if you hate them or don't have one or both, just cut the apple as close to the core as you can. If you do use one, spray it with canola oil first to make it easier to get the core out of the corer once it's cored (say that five times fast).

VEGAN WITH A VENGEANCE

Pear and Cranberry Tart

This is a really pretty tart, golden pears studded with burgundy cranberries. It's also low in sugar. Arrange the pear slices all in the same direction for a really professional look. You'll need a 9-inch tart pan with a removable bottom for this recipe. If you don't have one, you can use a pie plate.

FOR THE CRUST:
> ¼ cup slivered almonds
>
> 1 cup all-purpose flour
>
> ¼ teaspoon salt
>
> 3 tablespoons cold rice milk
>
> ¼ cup canola oil

FOR THE FILLING:
> 4 Bosc pears, peeled, cored, cut in half lengthwise then sliced lengthwise into ¼-inch-thick slices
>
> ¼ cup sugar
>
> 2 tablespoons arrowroot
>
> 1 tablespoon finely chopped crystallized ginger
>
> ¼ cup fresh cranberries, sliced in half
>
> ½ teaspoon almond extract
>
> 1 tablespoon water
>
> 1 teaspoon ground cinnamon
>
> ½ teaspoon freshly grated nutmeg

Prepare the crust:

Heat a small skillet over medium heat for 2 minutes. Place the slivered almonds in the pan and heat until golden brown, stirring often for 3 to 5 minutes. Transfer to a blender or food processor and pulse the toasted almonds to a fine powder.

In a large mixing bowl, sift together the flour, ground almonds, and salt. Sprinkle on the rice milk and oil and stir together with a fork. Form the dough into a ball and flatten into a disk. Wrap in plastic wrap and refrigerate for half an hour.

Preheat oven to 375°F. Place the chilled dough between two sheets of waxed paper. Roll into a 10-inch circle. Peel off the top layer of paper and place the dough paper side up in a tart pan. Remove the top sheet of paper and use your fingers to press the dough into the bottom and sides of the pan. Remove any excess dough so the top edges of the dough are flush with the top of the pan.

For the filling:

Combine the pears, sugar, arrowroot, crystallized ginger, fresh cranberries, almond extract, water, cinnamon, and nutmeg. Toss gently to combine the ingredients. Layer the pear mixture in the tart shell, evenly distributing the cranberries as you go. If there is some liquid left over, pour it in as well. Cover the pan with foil and bake at 375°F for 30 minutes. Remove the foil and bake 15 minutes more. Remove from oven and let cool before serving.

PUNK POINTS

To easily core pears, cut in half and use a measuring teaspoon to remove the seeds.

VEGAN WITH A VENGEANCE

Strawberry Shortcakes

Get a big forkful of the scone soaked in the strawberry sauce with a touch of the Macadamia Crème and it is just, do I say "heavenly" too often? Well, it's heavenly.

> Scones (page 42)
> Macadamia Crème (recipe follows)

> FOR THE STRAWBERRY SAUCE:
> 2 pounds strawberries, hulled and sliced (should come to about 7 cups)
> ½ cup sugar
> 1 tablespoon pure maple syrup
> 1 teaspoon vanilla extract

Make the sauce before making the scones and crème because the strawberries need to sit for an hour.

Place all the sauce ingredients in a bowl, stirring to make sure all the strawberries are coated with sugar. Cover and chill for at least an hour; the strawberries will develop a sauce on their own. That's all there is to making the sauce.

Split open the scones, spoon in some of the strawberry sauce (¼ cup or so per scone), cover, and dollop on some Macadamia Crème. Add a few more sliced strawberries to the top, serve.

Macadamia Crème

Takes five minutes to make, several hours to chill. I use this crème on puddings or on desserts with fruit toppings, including pancakes and waffles. It is easily modified by adding a touch of cinnamon or zest of orange or lemon. It's not fluffy like whipped cream, but it does taste just as good. Try it on Chocolate Pudding (page 244).

> ½ cup roasted macadamias (see Punk Points)
> ¼ cup soy milk
> ¼ cup confectioners' sugar
> ½ teaspoon vanilla extract
> ½ cup canola oil

In a food processor or strong blender, pulverize the roasted macadamias to form a fine powder. Add the soy milk and blend to form a thick paste. Add the confectioners' sugar and vanilla, and blend again. Add the oil in a steady stream while blending. The mixture will resemble a thick liquid. Transfer to a container with a tight lid or a bowl covered in plastic wrap, and chill for several hours, preferably overnight.

PUNK POINTS

If you can't find roasted macadamias that aren't salted, place raw macadamias on a baking sheet in a 350°F oven for 8 minutes, flipping them after 4 minutes. Or, buy roasted salted ones and rinse the salt off and pat dry.

VEGAN WITH A VENGEANCE

Strawberry-Rhubarb-Peach Pie

Ah, the bounties of spring. This is an obvious pie to make when the farmers' market is overflowing with luscious strawberries, juicy peaches, and tart rhubarb.

> 2 cups strawberries, sliced ¼ inch thick
> 1 cup peaches, pitted, peeled, and sliced ½ inch thick (see Punk Points, page 243)
> 2 cups rhubarb stalks, sliced ½ inch thick (discard all leaves; they are poisonous)
> ⅓ cup sugar
> ¼ teaspoon ground cardamom
> ½ teaspoon ground cinnamon
> 2 tablespoons tapioca starch or arrowroot or cornstarch
> ¼ cup maple syrup

Divide the pie crust dough in slightly unequal halves and roll out each crust into a disk onto parchment paper. The smaller crust should be the diameter of the top of your baking pan; the larger one should be a few inches wider to allow for the pan's depth plus a ½-inch overhang all around. Chill until ready to use.

Preheat oven to 425°F.

Line a 9-inch pie pan with the larger disk of pastry dough, allowing ½ inch of crust to hang over the edges of the pan.

Place the fruit and rhubarb in a mixing bowl and add the sugar and spices, mixing to distribute the sugar. Sprinkle in the tapioca starch, mix to incorporate, then add the maple syrup and mix again. Transfer to the pastry-lined pie pan.

Take the top crust and place it face down on top the pie; peel back the parchment paper. Fold the overhanging bottom crust back over the edges of the top crust and crimp the pastry together with your thumb and forefinger. Bake for 20 minutes, then reduce the heat to 350°F and bake for 25 to 30 minutes, or until the crust is golden and the juices are bubbling; let cool for a few hours before serving.

VEGAN WITH A VENGEANCE

Peach Cobbler

FOR THE FILLING:
- 8 peeled and sliced fresh peaches (makes about 5 cups)
- ¾ cup brown sugar
- 1 teaspoon ground cinnamon
- 2 teaspoons vanilla extract
- 2 tablespoons tapioca starch or arrowroot or cornstarch

FOR THE COBBLER TOPPING:
- 1 cup all-purpose flour
- 1½ teaspoons baking powder
- 1 teaspoon ground cinnamon
- ½ teaspoon ground allspice
- ¼ cup brown sugar, plus extra
  for sprinkling on crust
- ¼ cup vegetable oil
- ⅔ cup rice or soy milk
- 1 teaspoon vanilla extract

Preheat oven to 450°F and have ready a 9 × 13-inch baking dish—preferably Pyrex or ceramic.

Prepare the filling:
Mix all filling ingredients in the baking dish, set aside.

PUNK POINTS

To peel peaches, quickly blanch them in boiling water for about 45 seconds, then remove with a slotted spoon, cool, and peel. I am all for laziness and the energy you spend blanching will save you a ton of energy trying to peel the peaches without blanching.

Prepare the topping:
In a medium-size mixing bowl, sift together all the dry ingredients; create a well in the center, add the liquid ingredients, and mix with a wooden spoon until just combined. Drop by tablespoonfuls over the filling, leaving an inch or two of peaches between each spoonful. Sprinkle a little extra brown sugar over the top.
Bake for about 30 minutes, until the filling is bubbling and the top is browned.

DESSERTS

VEGAN WITH A VENGEANCE

Chocolate Pudding

Pudding is the ultimate comfort food for me. This is a fast, yummy, and satisfying treat that you can make with ingredients you probably have on hand. Try the variations below, and top with Macadamia Crème (page 240).

> 2 cups soy milk
> 3 tablespoons arrowroot or tapioca starch
> ½ cup sugar
> ⅓ cup cocoa powder
> 1 teaspoon vanilla extract
> ⅛ teaspoon almond extract

In a small saucepan off the heat whisk together the soy milk and arrowroot until the arrowroot is dissolved. Add the sugar and cocoa powder. Place over medium heat and whisk constantly until the mixture thickens, about 7 minutes. Once the mixture starts to bubble and is quite thick, turn the heat off. Mix in the extracts. Ladle the pudding into four wineglasses or ramekins, and chill in fridge for at least an hour and up to overnight. If you're leaving them in the fridge overnight, don't forget to cover them with plastic wrap once they are chilled, to prevent a skin from forming.

VARIATIONS

Chocolate Orange Pudding: Omit the almond extract; add along with the vanilla 1½ tablespoons of finely grated orange zest (between 1 and 2 oranges) and 1 tablespoon of orange liqueur.

Chocolate Coconut Pudding: Replace 1 cup of the soy milk with 1 cup of coconut milk, omit the almond extract, and add 1 teaspoon of coconut extract; sprinkle with shredded coconut after pouring into wineglasses.

Also, try adding ½ cup chopped walnuts or other nuts.

VEGAN WITH A VENGEANCE

Mexican Chocolate Rice Pudding

In Mexico, cinnamon is often used to enhance the flavor of chocolate, as if chocolate needs enhancing (but I have to admit that cinnamon and chocolate do taste good together). This creamy dessert is a nice ending to any Latin meal—it's impressive and unexpected while being ridiculously easy. Serve chilled in a wide-mouthed wineglass, or a small bowl, topped with Macadamia Crème (see page 240).

> 1 cup sushi or arborio rice, rinsed
> 1½ cups water
> 2 cups soy milk
> ¼ cup cocoa powder
> ¼ teaspoon ground cinnamon
> 2 ounces semisweet chocolate
> ⅓ cup pure maple syrup
> 1 teaspoon vanilla extract

Place the rinsed rice, water, and 1½ cups of the soy milk in a small saucepan, cover, and bring to a boil. Lower heat and cook at a low simmer for 10 minutes, until the rice is mostly cooked.

Add the cocoa, cinnamon, and semisweet chocolate, and stir until well combined and the chocolate is melted. Add the remaining ½ cup of soy milk, and the maple syrup and vanilla. Stir constantly for 5 minutes; if it looks too thick add a little more soy milk.

Remove from heat and let sit until it is at room temperature, then cover with platic wrap and chill for an hour and serve.

DESSERTS

VEGAN WITH
VENGEANCE

VEGAN WITH A VENGEANCE

VEGAN WITH A VENGEANCE

VEGAN WITH VENGEANCE

INDEX

VEGAN WITH A
VENGEANCE

VEGAN WITH A VENGEANCE

INDEX

Isa's back with a vengeance . . . and more dessert!

VEGAN CUPCAKES
TAKE OVER THE WORLD

*75 Dairy-Free Recipes for
Cupcakes That Rule*

by Isa Chandra Moskowitz
and Terry Romero
Hosts of the Post Punk Kitchen

176 pages | 35 color photos | $15.95 paper | 978-1-56924-273-5

Marlowe & Company
Available wherever books are sold
www.marlowepub.com
www.theppk.com

VEGAN WITH A VENGEANCE